Not everything is as it seems, and not everything that seems is.

Apocalyptin

First published 2022

ISBN: 9798846922495

Apocalyptin

From the Author

One of the most difficult challenges people have to overcome is forgiveness. Especially when someone has caused us unbearable pain and has severely hurt us, forgiveness often fails, even if we wish and make efforts to forgive after reading inspiring books, watching videos, and so on. Most often we forgive temporarily, and resentment returns. Most people live with resentment their whole life because they never managed to get rid of it, thus limiting their capabilities or often completely depriving themselves of any opportunities, and suffering from serious illnesses, failures, and other troubles and misfortunes. Resentment, together with other negative destructive emotions, blocks the circulation of energy, well-being, happiness, and health.

Like most people, I had to deal with pain and subsequent resentment so often throughout life. Resentment brought me to experience initial signs of cancer. All the existing books I read on the subject helped only temporarily. I therefore spent years studying many modalities of psychology, neuro-

linguistic programming (NLP) tools, energy practic-
es, and much more in search of truly effective tools for
getting rid of resentment as well as such destructive
emotions as anger, hatred, fear, sadness, depression,
and hopelessness. All that is needed to resolve such
emotions is explained in this book. All the stories of
childhood trauma are real stories of different people.
Apocalyptin is a fast medicine that helps. As far
as the form of presentation goes: it is not a familiar
one, and the narration itself can cause resistance. I ad-
vise you to be patient and don't stop reading the story
till the end. There are only 187 pages. I did my best to
keep the story as short and as effective as possible. It
is a psychotherapeutic tale and written according to
all the rules of this type of therapy. It contains all the
necessary tools and techniques for a maximum healing effect, working with the reader's subconscious. So
even if you feel like something doesn't make sense,
just trust the method and keep reading. Most important is emotionally and physically to feel everything the characters feel, which is described in detail.
You can also reread the story again and again, using
it like therapy. If I had the opportunity to read a book
like mine when I was in resentment and suffering, I
would have been very grateful for the effect and the
time saved. I really hope Apocalyptin will help everyone who reads it. I wrote it for that exact purpose.

Chapter 1

Odi awoke with a start. A loud scream pierced the air, followed by what sounded like a stampede coming down the hall towards his bedroom door.

"Come here, you lying, cheating bitch!" A loud slap followed. His mother was weeping—begging him to stop.

"I know you saw your lover today!"

Thirteen-year-old Odi pulled the pillow over his head and groaned. They were at it again. His mom and stepfather were fighting. Every time his stepfather got drunk, he made up stories to provoke fights with his mother, sometimes beating her up pretty badly, which happened often.

Odi hated, resented, and was terrified of his stepfather. He shuttered at the memory of the beatings he and his brother had taken over the years trying to protect their mother. They'd learned the hard way to stay out of it. Once, his stepfather was so wasted that he sprained Odi's arm trying to grab him. Mom never protected them—even worse, she scolded them for getting in the way and bothering her "lovely" husband. She even defended his stepfather when the cops came.

Another crash sounded in the hallway, and something hit the wall. He squeezed his eyes shut and could feel the hot tears of shame on his face. Yep, he was in for a long, sleepless night.

Odi's real father had left when he and his brother, Dan, were toddlers. So mom was, naturally—desperate. She had to find a second job to feed herself and her two young children. She'd drop them off at daycare early in the morning and pick them up late in the evening. By the time they got home, she was barely breathing from exhaustion. But despite all her efforts, there was little money, and even that was only enough for them to live a meager existence.

They were impoverished and lived in need all the time. The only reason they hadn't ended up on the streets already was because their mother owned the apartment where they lived. She'd inherited it from his grandma. His mom, who was always nervous and irritated, began to feed them randomly and behave strangely. Only as Odi grew older did he realize that his mother was drunk every night.

They lived like that for two years. Then one day, Sam appeared in their lives—he just showed up in their apartment one evening. After Dad left, he was the only man who'd paid any attention to their mother. He was tall and good-looking but utterly worthless, nasty, and rude to everyone. A real damn tool. He'd just been released from prison and only needed a place to stay. So he settled in from the first day. His exhausted mother, desperate to have any man fall in love with her, believed she was lucky to have him.

Sam immediately took on the role of master of the house. He said he'd put things in order from the very first day. By "order," he meant the most comfortable life for himself.

He never tried to hide his disdain and resentment of the two young boys. Sam was not shy about hurting them and treated them worse than animal abusers treat their dogs. Soon their stepfather switched from mental to physical abuse and used Odi and his brother as punching bags. Odi had just turned four, and his brother, Dan, six.

Their mom was sure that this "amazing man" was her only chance and allowed him to do whatever he wanted. So she tried to please her lover and shush the boys.

Sam seemed to delight in causing the boys to feel insecure and miserable, and as a result, they started to hate Sam and their mother.

Within six months, Sam and his mother were married, and the boys felt total and utter despair, realizing that he had settled in with them for the long haul. Sam's only desire was for them to disappear and let him enjoy his life.

That had been nine years ago.

As the rantings of his stepfather and desperate screams of his mother continued to rage outside his door, Odi thought, *Luckily, I locked my door from the inside this time.* Sometimes, when his stepfather chased his mother around the house, they'd break into Odi's or his brother's bedroom.

Odi was trembling under his blanket from anxiety and exhaustion and felt little fingers of fear trickle down his spine. He was ashamed that he was still experiencing those creepy feelings at the age of thirteen. He hated himself for that.

Odi flinched as a glass object shattered against his door. He felt his stomach lurch. He used to feel sorry for his mom, but over the years, he'd watched her play the victim card far too often and was now convinced that she enjoyed being one.

Odi sighed, he didn't want to be a victim, but he didn't want to become a murder statistic either. On the contrary, he was convinced that as soon as he got a little older, he'd be able to run away. He just needed to get enough money for that—even if he had to steal it. He thought about that a lot. He was already looking for an opportunity. Then no one would ever be able to humiliate him again. He looked out the window—It was getting light—another sleepless night.

Odi waited until an hour after the fight had subsided to start getting ready for school. It was a gloomy morning. He thought he'd make some toast and tea (bread and water like in prison) and stared out the kitchen window. It looked like it was going to rain. "Shit!" Odi shouted indignantly. He didn't like the rain because his sneakers were leaking. He shivered; there was a cold draft coming from somewhere.

"Hey, when are you going to get out of here? My friends are coming over soon, and we don't want to see you around here."

Odi nearly jumped out of his skin. It was his older brother, Dan.

He may have managed to hide from his stepfather occasionally but could never escape his brother's bullying whenever they were together. Odi let out a heart-felt sigh. He remembered last fall, when their neighbor, Gill, had beat him up so severely that he lost his memory and couldn't recall what had happened (he was found unconscious near their apartment).

Instead of defending him, his brother called him a weakling. Odi had become a stranger in his own home, especially after his brother figured out how to make friends with their stepfather. Dan was already reaping those rewards. Odi looked down at his brother's new sneakers.

Dan saw where Odi's eyes had wandered and wiggled his sneakers at him. "Oh, do you like my new shoes?" Then, laughing, he ridiculed him. "Don't worry, little bro, once they become too worn and torn for me, I'll be sure and give them to you. He snapped his fingers. I've got connections around here now, you know."

Odi stared down at his thread-bare tee-shirt and jeans. He'd been wearing his brother's old, worn-out clothes and stinky shoes all his life. A tear trickled down his cheek before he could stop it. And for that, Odi started to hate his brother. He swiped away the tear with a vengeance. With *Dan's new ally—his stepfather- he knew he was destined to wear hand-me-down clothes and old shoes forever!*

Odi angrily brushed past his smirking brother on his way out. Everyone wanted to break him and try to destroy him—within the walls of his own home—every day! He felt hopeless and sure the world was a cruel, disgusting place, where everyone was waiting for him to trip up and fall headfirst against the pavement, squishing his brain. But in the meantime, they made sure they used him, lied to him, and constantly dragged him into some kind of trouble.

Even on his way home from school, Odi often suffered from the anticipation of what he might find when he got home. It made him dizzy sometimes. He

5

never knew what awaited him. What mood would his stepfather be in today? Maybe it would be a good day, and he'd be able to get some sleep, or perhaps the yelling and fighting would wake him again, and if he intervened, he'd get in trouble for sure.

He was undoubtedly alone in this world, and his only way to survive was to fight. Unfortunately, that was prevalent here. He'd give them payback for every knock since the very first one. Odi raised his fist angrily and shouted, "Someday, I'll get even with all of you." He shook his fist at the room. "I curse you all!" Odi was numb with anger, and his mouth was as dry as a desert. He sloshed down the rest of his tea, slammed the cup on the counter, grabbed his jacket, and left for school.

Chapter 2

While Odi walked to school, he noticed a young boy walking on the opposite side of the street. Actually, the kid saw him first. He stared at Odi without even blinking. The boy was wearing a gray T-shirt and blue jeans, and for some reason, he was barefoot. His T-shirt was torn, and he was crying. Odi glanced at him and kept on walking.

As Odi continued his way to school, he thought about the young boy he'd seen. What was the little one doing out walking the streets alone? Odi remembered seeing the child's tears. He hated tears; for him, it was a sign of weakness. He felt nausea overtake him. The kid reminded him too much of himself when he was young. "Not my business." He was determined to keep walking, forcing himself not to look back.

The first one to greet Odi at school was Big Jake, a harmless character in general but quite a bully when angered, mostly attacking his weaker schoolmates. It was apparent that Jake was having a bad day, and Odi wanted to avoid him at all costs, but Jake forcefully bumped into him, shoving him into the opposite hallway wall.

"Hey, watch your step, you scum!" Big Jake barked, but Odi was already gone, hiding behind the corner, trying to catch his breath, when he bumped into Dina.

"Why are you hiding, dude? Dina whispered conspiratorially. "What happened?" Dina was also 13 and his best and only friend since fourth grade. His BFF.

"Nothin.' I was running late this morning," Odi replied, not liking her tone.

"Sure. Look what I finally pinched from my mom," Dina said, showing him a tiny pouch.

"Put it away, Dina," Odi hissed.

"Oh, don't be such a drag! Aren't you gonna try it with me? I can't wait to get crunked! She waved the pouch in his face. "Come on, let's have a little fun before class; let's share some real danger!" Dina said playfully.

That's the last thing I need, Odi thought. *I have too much danger in my life already.* He looked into Dina's eyes. "Dina, do you want to become like her?"

"Like whom?" Dina pretended not to understand the question.

"Like your mother!" Odi raised his voice, forgetting that someone might hear them.

Dina's expression changed. "Oh yeah? Well, look at your own! She isn't any better!" she grunted, ready to leave.

Odi took her hand in his.

"What now?" Dina looked down. She didn't want him to see her sudden tears. She knew he hated tears.

He squeezed her hands. "Just put it away, ok?

Let's not complicate things."

"No!"

Odi dropped her hands. "This is such bullshit. You don't even know what this is."

"My life is more than complicated! My life is a nightmare, and my father is the monster!" She let out a sob. "I couldn't even look at myself in the mirror this morning." She looked at Odi through tear-stained eyes, her eye makeup running in black streaks down her cheeks. "He came into my room again last night!" She sobbed. "Mother came in and caught him, but she pretended not to notice anything." Dina put her face in her hands. "Now, I've become his dirty little whore, and if anyone finds out, they'll never treat me well. She stared at Odi with laser focus. "Do you promise never to tell anyone?"

Odi threw up his hands. "Of course, I promise not to tell anyone, silly. And you are not a whore. Your dad is an animal!"

Tears flashed in her eyes again. Only this time, she pursed her lips and held them back. Clenching her teeth in anger, she said. "It's ok; he doesn't know what's going to happen to him when I grow up. I will be his judge and jury ... I will cut off his tool myself ... he has no idea who he is dealing with!"

Dina's fists were clenched so hard that her knuckles turned white, and she couldn't hold back anymore. A tear slid down her cheek. She hastily wiped it off with her finger, trying to be tough.

Odi felt sorry for her. He'd known about her, "dirty little secret," as she called it, from the moment it started. Anger and hatred overwhelmed him. He was going to help her punish that sonofabitch! His clenched fists made his nails dig deep, half-moon marks, into his palms.

Dina stayed silent with her head down.

"Come on, Dina," Odi said, patting her hand. "I'll walk you home after school, and we'll get some beer and chill out at our place. But please throw that shit away, ok?"

Dina sighed. "Deal. Let's go get sloshed, at least," Dina answered as they walked into their respective classrooms.

Chapter 3

T he school day was over. Odi looked for Dina
but couldn't find her. After a while, he thought
that maybe she'd decided to go straight to their
secret place without him. It was just a boarded-up gazebo amidst overgrown trees in a park. But to them,
it was their secret shelter—their safe haven. There
were old, dilapidated benches inside that they'd set
up and made comfortable. They'd spent a lot of time
there over the years, hanging out and drinking the
beer they'd managed to steal from a local warehouse.

Odi hurried to get there.

When he arrived at the gazebo, Dina wasn't
around. He called her cell, but she didn't answer. So
finally, after waiting and calling her for over an hour,
he decided to jog to her house, praying nothing terrible had happened to her.

On his way there, Odi ran into the same kid. This
time the kid hailed him as soon as he saw him. Odi
waited for a second, then hesitantly walked over to
him. "What do you need, kiddo?" Odi asked him.

The boy looked at him with big, sad eyes. "Please

help me. He's looking for me and wants to punish me!" the boy cried.

Odie scanned the area. "What? Who is going to punish you? What for?"

"There ..." the boy sniffled, pointing at the house down the street.

Suddenly Odi noticed a huge man approaching them from that direction and thought his knees might buckle. His heart sank, and he started breathing heavily, regretting he'd gotten involved. The guy glared at Odi. The kid slipped in behind him.

The giant was getting closer.

"Hey, boy! Get away from that kid. He's mine!" the giant yelled.

"What do you mean yours?" Odi replied, not recognizing his own voice. It sounded quite firm.

Odi thought it ought to sound fearful.

"That's exactly what I mean!" The giant let out an evil growl and was now only about fifty feet away.

Odi had to act fast. Fear made him remember all the tricks he'd learned from action movies. He knew he wouldn't win the fight, so he grabbed the kid and ran as fast as he could, carrying the little boy in his arms.

The giant was dumbfounded and started running after them, cursing. But he was too drunk and clumsy to catch Odi.

Chapter 4

The little boy held on tight to Odi's jacket as he ran, desperately looking for a gateway or somewhere to hide from the predator. He finally turned at the first corner and noticed a slightly open door, instantly realizing he had never seen an entry here before. It was unclear where it would lead, but there was no time to contemplate it. It was a chance he'd have to take.

They slipped through the door, and Odi instinctively bolted it shut. He set the kid on the floor and leaned against the wall, sliding down it, his breathing labored. Everything around him had suddenly become quiet, dank, and dusky. He couldn't understand where the tiny sliver of light was coming from. It felt weird here, in this building, because the time of day seemed different.

His temples were pounding, and he could hardly see or hear anything. He'd become nauseous, and there was a buzzing noise in his ears. He closed his eyes. He had never run so fast in his life, especially carrying the heavy burden of a child.

Finally, Odi caught his breath and opened his eyes. The little kid was gone, and Odi was now in the middle of a dark hallway. *How did I get here? And what's happened to the time? Why had it suddenly become so dark? Where had the kid vanished to? And how would he find his way home without bumping into that drunken giant?*

Odi stood, took a couple of steps, and noticed a man slumped against a wall on the opposite side of the hallway. It was difficult to see the man's face in the dark. He seemed distracted and hadn't noticed Odi, who unconsciously swallowed his thick saliva and turned back to the door he'd just entered to escape. It was gone!

"Shit!" There seemed to be no way out of the building. Realizing that, Odi froze in horror. His heart pounded. As he contemplated a way to pass the man unnoticed, he saw an arch that looked like it could get him back onto the street. Then he'd be able to get out of this mess and look for Dina. He was very worried about her.

Like a panther, he crouched low and slowly and carefully started moving toward the arch. He was almost there when he glanced at the man.

He froze in horror. It was his neighbor, that guy, Gill, the same man who'd beaten him up so badly last summer. Gill was twenty and a major slacker who lived three floors above them. This guy always hung around, just looking to start a fight. Odi couldn't stand the bastard. Over the years, he'd taken Odi's temper to the limit. Now he was sorry he hadn't grabbed the kitchen knife that morning, even though he'd thought about it. If this guy noticed him, that would surely be the end of Odi.

But the guy didn't move. It appeared that his neighbor was asleep against the wall. *Oh ... he's just passed out drunk,* thought Odi with relief. Then he noticed the neighbor was wearing a pair of blue jeans and a torn gray T-shirt, and he was barefoot, just like the little kid who'd gotten Odi involved in this mess in the first place, then disappeared.

What did it all mean?

Odi worried that he'd lost his mind. He had just run a mile carrying a kid in his arms, and now he had to deal with his awful neighbor.

Chapter 5

Night had fallen, even though in Odi's mind, it was only the middle of the day. Someone tugged on Odi's sleeve. Frightened, he spun around, ready to fight. And there stood the same little kid he'd rescued. "Oh, there you are!" Odi said. He again noticed that the kid wore the same clothes as Gill and was barefoot. In response, the kid held out a flashlight towards Odi's face, persistently wiggling it at him while nodding at the flashlight.

Odi pushed it away. "My friend, I know it's gotten dark, but I'll manage to find my way home without the flashlight, believe me," whispered Odi. "Thank you, but keep it. You'll make better use of it." Odi patted the little boy's head. "You know what? I need to take you home."

The kid stared at Odi with wide eyes, still holding the flashlight out to him as if desperate for him to take it.

Odi finally did. "Thank you, but what should I do with it?"

"Flash the light on him," whispered the kid,

pointing at the barefoot neighbor, who was still sitting there quietly, and it seemed, still passed out.

As if moving in slow motion, Odi directed the flashlight beam at his neighbor, hearing a voice shouting in his head. *Odi! What are you doing? You're going to wake him up!*

Odi's heart was pounding, his forehead covered in sweat. He knew something was going to happen now, but he couldn't stop himself. He wanted to take off and run away when the flashlight beam caught the neighbor's belly. And Odi saw something he'd remember for the rest of his life.

The man's body had become transparent, and a strange, gray box was inside him. Odi couldn't believe his eyes. His mouth fell open in astonishment.

The little kid turned to Odi. "You saved me today. I will always remember that." Then he walked over to Gill and, pulling on the edges of the box, climbed inside Gill's body.

Frightened, Odi dropped the flashlight. The sound of it hitting the ground made a loud clanging noise. The beam from the flashlight jumped in the darkness, casting eerie shadows on the surrounding walls. Other than that, he was in total darkness.

The neighbor and the kid had disappeared into the darkness. Only a thin beam of light came from the flashlight lying on the floor, pointing to Odi's right. He rushed to grab it.

Chapter 6

"**G**ood job, boy!" exclaimed someone standing next to him in the darkness.

Odi jumped from fright. He snatched the flashlight from the floor and aimed it toward the voice like a weapon in case it was his neighbor. But instead, the flashlight illuminated on a lone figure. Odi saw a boy before him (Odi's age), leaning against the wall, with his arms folded across his chest, smiling at him.

Odi immediately looked to where the neighbor and kid had just been in case he needed help, but they had disappeared. "What the hell? Who are you?" Odi stammered. He was already stunned by everything that had happened, and now he was staring at yet another stranger.

The teen wore a pair of dress pants and a shirt. But his clothes were shiny and - GOLD! Who could afford to buy that in this neighborhood?

The golden boy said, "Odi, you have no idea what just happened, do you? You passed the test! This is a great beginning for the new change!" the stranger said excitedly moving closer to Odi. As he did, some of his limbs illuminated.

Odi waved the flashlight menacingly at him. What test?" he asked, confused.

The teen shaded his eyes with his palms. "The most important one."

"Which is?" Odi's eyes bored into those of the teen. "And how do you know my name?"

"For God's sake, quit waving that flashlight in my face." He pushed Odi's flashlight away. "I know everything about you. That's how it is supposed to be."

Since golden boy was his size, Odi didn't get scared; he got mad. *Ha! Some glamor guy is standing here talking shit about changing me. There's nothing wrong with me. Why he should have seen me running away from that massive guy with a kid in my arms.*

"Odi," the golden boy continued, "you were courageous. You have a huge heart. I knew you would manage; I just didn't know how well. I am so proud of you!" He bowed at the waist.

"What? Me? What the f—. Why didn't you help me before if you were here?" Odi snapped. "Were you afraid to soil your fancy clothes?"

Golden boy's face grew serious. "Why do you think I didn't help?"

Odi looked again at the wall where the neighbor had been. *Had that happened?* Had he really seen inside his neighbor's body? Odi was confused. He looked at the flashlight. Maybe it was magical—it had to be—but if he told anyone, they'd think he was crazy. "Listen, how did you get here?" Odi turned to the golden boy, but no trace of him was left. *Nice chat …*

Odi glanced around. He was alone. The flashlight in his hand was the only actual proof of the encounter with the young child and the golden boy. Odi was trying to make sense of it all. Could it have been his imagination? The flashlight was real, though. Then, completely confused, he remembered Dina. He shoved the flashlight into his back pocket and ran away through the arch.

Chapter 7

It was sunny and light again on the other side of the building. Everything was the same as before he'd opened that door; only everything seemed brighter. Odi rubbed his eyes. He smelled freshly baked bread and heard some happy music coming from somewhere. He took a deep breath, enjoying the delicious aroma. He hadn't eaten anything since early that morning. He looked back and saw only a wall—the arch was no longer there. Strange.

He was baffled. Could it have all been a dream? No, his arms still hurt from carrying the kid while running away from the predator. Then he remembered the flashlight tucked in the back pocket of his jeans. The flashlight was there. That meant everything that had happened was real!

He thought, *at least I have something interesting to tell Dina.* He knew she would never believe he was crazy. "Dina! I still have to find her!" He pulled his phone out of his jacket pocket and called her number again. No answer. "Damn … this is not good."

A child's cry interrupted Odi's train of thought.

The cry was coming from around the corner of the building. He followed the sound. He knew there was a small, old, abandoned playground there.

Walking quickly, he looked around the corner. On the playground were a little girl and a big guy. The girl tried to hold onto a flower with all her might while the guy tried to grab it from her. The girl was sobbing, desperately trying to get away from him. But the playground was fenced in a circle with an iron grid, so the girl was trapped like a caged animal and unable to escape.

Odi felt her fear and shame from afar and crouched low behind a tree to get a closer look. It was a bizarre scene. He had no idea why some big guy would want to take a flower from a little girl. But he knew one thing for sure; the little one was terrified. She held one hand out as if to ward him off and kept covering the flower with her free hand as if protecting it like it was something very precious.

"Please no … Please no … Please, no," the little girl pleaded with shame, exhaustion pulling her to her knees.

The big guy didn't seem to care and seemed to be having fun as he mockingly laughed at her. Then, finally, he came to stand over her, casting an evil shadow over her meager body as she knelt before him. "Come on, girly! Give it to me!

To Odi, she was powerless, the situation hopeless, and there was no one to protect her. She was crying desperately.

Something clenched in Odi's stomach. He looked around in search of help. There was no one around. *Where had everyone gone today? Nobody is around at all,* he thought. *What shall I do? I can't deal with that big guy. Shit! I could care less … none of my business … I mustn't interfere …*

The girl began to wail even louder. Odi flinched. He physically felt her terror and despair. Suddenly, something clicked inside him, and he didn't like what he was thinking. *Odi, have you lost your mind? He's three times bigger than you! Odi was torn between running or interceding.* Then, unexpectedly, even for himself, Odi yelled, "Hey, dude! Get away from her! She's just a baby!"

Immediately he regretted it.

But it was already too late. The big guy flinched and blinked a few times as if coming out of a trance. He glared at Odi.

Oh, shit! Odi thought.

Chapter 8

"**A**re you talking to me, you little puke? Get the hell out of here while you still can!" the big guy shouted.

That was Odi's only chance to run away, but he just couldn't do it. It had always been inherent in him; he was always eager to champion the weak and the helpless. "I ain't goin' nowhere! Let her go!" Odi stated loudly and firmly. He could feel his heart pounding with fear. Yet, at the same time, he felt sorry for the girl and was very angry with that guy for having the nerve to attack a child over a flower. *What am I doing? He'll make minced meat out of me now.*

The big guy shook his fist at Odi. "Oh really? Then you're dead meat!" he shouted and rushed to the gate.

Suddenly ominous dark clouds covered the sun chasing away the blue sky. Thunder rumbled overhead, and an angry wind-whipped dust and trash all over the playground.

Odi was panic-stricken. Not only had it been a bizarre and long day, but it could also be the last day of his life! Everything got fuzzy and moved in slow motion. Odi looked up as if waiting for a sign from above to help him when he noticed a shimmering object floating in the air. He squinted to see what it was. It was a golden feather floating towards him. Without giving it any thought, Odi jumped and grabbed it.

Everything froze, including the big guy running full steam at him. The wind calmed, and debris froze as it twirled in the air. Everything, even the clouds, froze. Time was standing still. It was so quiet. Odi realized that the only thing he could hear was his heartbeat hammering in his chest.

He looked at the shimmering gold feather and remembered that he had the flashlight. He snatched it from his pocket and, already knowing what to do, turned it on and directed it toward the big guy. Inside his body, just like his neighbor's, in the same kind of box, sat a little boy. He was dressed exactly like the big guy, sitting there all curled up and confused, staring at Odi, his eyes squinting from the bright light.

Odi turned off the flashlight and put it in his back pocket, but even without it, he still saw the kid inside the box.

The kid quickly jumped out of the box and ran towards Odi. "Please, please don't hurt me! Please help me!" the child cried. The little boy took Odi's hand and stared straight into his eyes, his own full of tears. Odi felt sorry for the boy.

"What? How can I help you?" Odi asked in confusion.

"Just know that I'm there … nobody sees me, and nobody understands that I am there … nobody feels for me, but I am always there, and I am always crying," said the little one.

He ran back to the big guy, stopped, and looked at the frozen girl, who stood motionless. "I am very sorry; please forgive me if you can," the boy said, his voice raspy with tears. He climbed up on the big guy, still frozen, and got into the box inside him. He again looked pointedly at Odi, then disappeared inside.

Unexpectedly, everything came alive again. The wind picked up and blew the dark clouds away along with the dust and the trash. The sun peeked through puffy white clouds again, and the sky was blue once more. Odi managed to grab the golden feather floating in the air.

The big guy awoke and looked around in confusion.

The little girl was standing further away, wiping at her tears.

The big guy looked neither at Odi nor the girl he'd offended earlier. Instead, he just stared straight ahead with a dull look. Then he headed in the opposite direction and walked away.

Odi followed him with his eyes until he was gone, then changed his focus to the little girl. She was standing in the middle of the playground, holding her flower protectively. Now, when he looked at her with more attention, she looked familiar. "Everything is fine; you are safe now," he told her. "Come on; I'll walk you home." He started to walk to the gate, but the little girl whizzed past him.

She got to the entrance ahead of him and got out of the playground. She stopped for a second and glanced towards her assailant way up the street now. She turned to Odi and said, "Thank you, Odi! I knew you were special."

Odi peered closely at her trying to figure out how he knew her. Her way of talking and the looks she gave him seemed very familiar. "Listen, have I seen you before? What's your name?"

"Jenny!" the girl shouted and ran away as fast as she could.

"Mom?" Odi recalled the little girl he'd seen in old childhood photos of his mother. Odi was perplexed. But how? Why? This child was his mom when she was little!

Chapter 9

"Another job well done!" a familiar voice said.

Odi jumped and looked behind him. It was the golden boy again. "Oh, it's you, watching and not helping again." Odi gave him a dirty look.

"Not helping? Really?" The golden boy slid his sunglasses down his nose and peered over them at Odi. "You're being ungrateful." He pointed to the feather in Odi's hand. "That is mine. Would you please give it back to me?"

Odi looked at the glowing feather and pondered for a moment. "Why would I do that?" Odi asked innocently.

"Because it belongs to me. I sent it to you to help you take on that big guy, yet you keep saying I didn't help you," the golden boy said, turning his back on Odi in a huff.

That's when Odi saw his neat, tight-fitting wings. "Wha-?" Odi's mouth dropped open in astonishment. Then he shook it off and asked with a grin: "Why are you walking around in your Halloween costume?"

"My wings are real," the golden boy replied

sternly, flapping his brilliant, golden wings. "I'm your guardian angel. I wasn't just standing there, observing. I am unable to intervene except in an emergency. But, as you might have noticed, my feather helped you greatly." The angel quickly approached him without touching the ground and smiled as he extended his hand for Odi to shake.

Odi looked at the angel's hand as if it were a poisonous snake. He was not about to shake this weirdo's hand. However, his acquaintance didn't seem to mind.

The angel shrugged. "Alright, if you don't want to believe me—that's up to you, but I am your guardian angel. So please give me back my feather."

"Ok." Odi let go of the feather, and it floated towards the angel. But suddenly, he snatched it back in midair. "Wait!

The angel raised an eyebrow. "Wait?"

"Yes, let me keep it for a while. I think I might still need it."

"Are you sure?"

Odi rubbed the feather's stem between his thumb and forefinger, making it wiggle. "Yep.

The angel looked pensive. "I don't think I should. I … "

Odi whirled on him. "A guardian angel, you say? Isn't that like some kind of guard? Aren't you supposed to protect me all these times? Odi went to stand nose to nose with his guardian angel. "So, where the hell were you before?" Odi asked, "Like when everyone was beating the shit out of me all my life?"

The angel looked deep into Odi's eyes. There was so much anger and hate in them. "As you will, Odi. But I'm not just, as you say, watching you without helping," the angel angrily whispered and vanished into thin air.

"Bullshit!" Odi gazed at the space from where the angel had just disappeared. He shook his head in disbelief. He was so pissed off at that golden pimp's attitude that he was trembling. There was a loud buzzing in his ears. He desperately needed to lean against something or sit down to recover from everything that had just happened. So, he sat down in the street.

He was still trying to process what had happened with that little girl (his mom!). Then, he realized that something very offensive had happened to her. He suddenly felt very sorry for her and very angry with that big guy, but at the same time, he remembered the little kid inside that big galute. "Just remember that I am there," sounded in Odi's head. "Damm! This is so confusing!" *Everyone must have a little kid inside them*, he concluded.

Chapter 10

"Hey, you!"

Odi turned around. Was someone calling him? A lady was standing at the entrance of a coffee shop with a steaming cup in her hands. She was a tall, statuesque lady with glorious, dark hair. She wore a long, old-fashioned dress.

"Me?" Odi pointed to himself.

"Yes, you! Why are you sitting in the middle of the street? Come over here, and I will treat you to a cup of coffee! It looks like you've had a pretty rough day."

"A rough day," repeated Odi. "You have no idea."

Odi smelled the aromatic coffee. He was exhausted and hungry, so he didn't have to be asked twice. He headed toward the coffee shop.

The woman breathed in the steam and said, "The coffee is quite good. Come in, I will make you a cup just like this one. I think some fresh croissants could also be useful," she continued, gesturing for him to come inside.

Odi was almost to the doorstep when he suddenly stopped. Suspicious, he looked inside. The woman had gone behind the bar to stand next to the coffee machine. Odi yelled, "Listen, if any of you start anything, I can handle myself and you and your friends. Got it?"

As he nervously went inside, he realized the people sitting there were so old they wouldn't be able to catch him if he ran. So he stepped up to the bar and spoke to the lady. "Give me something a bit stronger if you're feeling generous."

Odi had lowered his voice to sound older and more confident. He wanted to appear cool and masculine in the presence of the beautiful lady. And he'd been through so much today that having a drink wouldn't hurt. He'd gotten used to drinking beer with Dina. And if he came home drunk, it would be easier to pass out and sleep until morning.

The lady smiled and looked straight into his eyes. "Coffee and croissants, boy!" The light illuminated the jewelry around her headpiece, an accessory he hadn't seen when they'd met. It shimmered right into his eyes.

Odi was taken with her beautiful face. She was wearing a very strange dress; it was more like a costume than a dress, really. With her crown, she looked like a queen of some sort.

What the hell is going on? Everyone seems to be wearing a costume today, he thought. He chuckled and plopped down on a chair at a table closest to the exit. Of course, one has to always keep their eyes open.

While the strange woman in the queen outfit fiddled with the coffee, Odi scanned the room. Everything seemed unusual here. He'd only seen decor like this in travel commercials. *Someday I, too, shall travel the world*, he thought

"Why would you wait? You're almost a grownup!" the woman said, approaching him. She put a cup of coffee and a plate of croissants in front of him.

"Did I say something out loud?" Odi asked.

"No! But you thought it," the woman replied with a sly smile. "Come on, have some food. You are very hungry," she said, nodding to the plate, then walked back to the bar.

Odi grabbed the croissants like a hungry lion devouring its prey. He hadn't eaten anything all day, and certainly nothing so tasty for a very long time. He chewed greedily and washed them down with the sweet, fragrant coffee.

The lady made another cup of coffee for herself and sat at the other table, looking at Odi. "So, did you have a rough day?" she asked, staring intently at him.

"Oh," He replied on a deep sigh. "You wouldn't believe the day I've had." Odi wrung his hands together in front of him. "This day has been so long and so damn strange." His gaze met hers across the table. "Do you believe we all have a guardian angel?"

The lady cocked her head to one side. "Of course we do! Why? Do you doubt it?" answered the lady.

Odi sighed. "Well, it seems that I have one, but he's too fancy to do his job! At least I got that impression from him!" Odi took the feather out of his pocket and wiggled it in front of the lady's face.

She shoved Odi's hand away. "No, no! Put that back at once!" The woman scanned their surroundings. Two older men were sitting in the back of the coffee shop, but no one was paying attention to them. Still, she didn't want anyone to see what Odi had in his hand.

"What's the big deal?" Odi tossed the gold feath-

33

er onto the table. "I'm always being accused of doing something wrong." He sighed deeply. "Who are you anyway?"

Odi examined her features closely. It seemed that they were changing right before his eyes. Her face was both old and young, but her eyes were those of a young girl. "Are you going to keep it a secret?" Odi asked again.

The woman took a sip of her coffee. "I am a fairy," she said.

Chapter 11

O di's eyes grew wide. "What? What do you
mean you're a fairy? Have you recently been released from a psycho ward? This is funny!" Odi
laughed. He'd rather laugh than be taken for a fool.

"Have you never heard of fairies, my friend?" the
woman answered firmly.

Now Odi realized she was not joking and consid-
ered herself a fairy. *Gosh, maybe she's high!*

Odi stood abruptly and threw his napkin on the
table. "Listen, I'm out of here!" he took a last sip of
coffee. He was angry and way ready to leave this
weird place. He'd had enough for today!

The lady came to stand in front of him and held
her hand up for him to stop. "Alright, calm down. I
am a fairy. I am looking after you, Odi."

"Looking after me?" Odi grew tense. "Another
keeper? How in the hell did I get so popular? In what
way are you looking after me, and for how long have
you been? And oh yeah, how do you know my name?"

"Well, I've known who you are for a long time,"
the fairy giggled. "And I don't always look like this,

but it's safer for me here. Alright, are you done with your coffee now? Want another one? It is decaf … less harmful."

"Thanks. So why would you be giving out free coffee to strangers? Do you want something from me? I don't sell any drugs, just so you know." *For now,* he thought.

She set her coffee cup in the saucer with a clatter. "Don't even think about selling drugs, young man." The fairy had read his mind again. "I'd like you to meet someone."

She stepped aside, and a young boy sat at the table.

"More kids!" Odi exclaimed, annoyed. Then he froze. The boy was wearing the same outfit as he was. Odi could already guess what that meant, although he had almost no childhood memories or photos.

"Are you. Are you … me … as little Odi?" he asked the young kid.

"Yes. Hi, Odi," the little one replied and smiled slightly. The fairy brought him a milkshake and a cookie.

For the first time today, the older Odi was speechless. He was looking at a clear picture of himself in his childhood. He didn't remember his father because he'd left when Odi was two years old. Odi never saw him again. The day his father left was the day his mom started channeling her anger on them and extinguishing it with alcohol. She was miserable, angry, and drunk all the time now. He hated her. He did.

But then he remembered the little girl with the flower on the playground. Now he had a pretty good picture of what had happened to her. Of course, not everything was crystal clear yet, but he was determined to figure it out. Now he felt for her, poor little girl.

"Odi, I want you to save me," the little Odi said, interrupting his thoughts. "You helped that guy ... your neighbor's inner kid."

"Wait ... What?" Odi threw up his arms. "Listen, I never intended to help anyone!" Odi cried out. "Especially our neighbor, Gill! It just worked out that way. Do you get it? Does anyone get it?" he shouted through the room. He was boiling mad and felt something snap inside him, something he couldn't stop. "I wish everyone would leave me alone. I have no desire to save anyone. No one ever saved me! For thirteen years, no one gave a crap about me! Not even that dushbag with the golden wings and smug smile! Where was he when I needed protection and help? So why should I care?"

Odi then turned on the fairy. "And what do you, a half-witted woman—know about life?"

He looked at the little Odie. "Listen, kid. I tried to hide the best I could. All I've done my whole life was trying to get out of that monster's way. But no matter how hard I tried, I never managed to escape his abuse!"

"I know, Odi, I was there!" the little boy cried, jumping off the chair. He pushed Odi and burst out sobbing.

"Ok, boys, cool down!" She hadn't said it loudly, but the windows shook in response.

The café turned deathly silent. The two old guys in the back of the coffee shop stopped talking and stared at the fairy. She locked eyes with one of them and motioned to the exit with her head. He nodded and hurried outside.

Chapter 12

"Now, you calm down right now, Odi." The fairy's eyes bored into the big Odi's. Then, when he plopped into a chair pouting, she said, "I have something to show you. Get your flashlight."

Odi leered at her. "How do you know about the flashlight? Are you and the kid in this, like some kind of sect? This is totally confusing shit!"

The fairy threw up her hands. "Of course not. I already told you I am a fairy; do you doubt my words?" The fairy made a dismissive wave of her hands. "Never mind, just give me the flashlight."

Odi squinted suspiciously and pulled the flashlight from his back pocket. Reluctantly, he handed it to her.

The fairy pushed it back at him. "No, you must hold it. Turn it on now and shine it over there on that wall."

Odi gave her a menacing look but didn't say a word. Instead, he walked over to the wall and aimed the flashlight at it.

Little Odi sat on the chair and continued to sip

his milkshake.

Suddenly, eerie shadows moved across the wall, then a real movie began. Odi was captivated. His mouth opened in amazement.

"Watch, Odi, and observe," the fairy said.

The movie began with a young man in a room filled with small electronics and machinery of all kinds strewn everywhere. He was a mechanical engineer. And the serious-minded people walking along helping him were engaged in something fascinating and clearly enjoyed their work. Odi observed them with curiosity and pleasure; he'd never seen such enthusiasm. He got carried away for a moment forgetting reality.

The movie about the engineer continued. The man had invented a fuel-efficient electric car based on his other invention: a machine that was extracting electricity from air which was a huge success, and his inventions made him very wealthy. Then the movie panned in on his happy family in their beautiful home, perfectly landscaped yard, and a garage full of expensive cars. His beautiful, happy wife sat at a huge dinner table with two well-dressed, cheerful children running around. The woman served a succulent, stuffed turkey. Odi thought he could smell it; so good.

Static appeared, and the movie turned into black and white. Now a completely different picture appeared that Odi was painfully familiar with. A drunken man was hitting his mother and then turned on him and his brother. He struck the boy. The child fell to the floor and couldn't get up. Odi felt a knot in his throat. His breathing quickened. His ears started ringing, and there was a buzzing noise in his head.

The flashlight fell out of his hand, hitting the floor with a loud clang.

The movie stopped. The silence that followed was deafening.

Little Odi started sobbing.

"What do you have to say?" the fairy asked.

Odi bent down, retrieved the flashlight, and thrust it into his back pocket. "What should I say," Odi replied over his shoulder on his way back to his table.

"What would you say about the first movie and the second?" replied the fairy, following him.

"The first one is a fairy tale, a Hollywood story! He's rich and successful. They're all beautiful, well-dressed, neat, and slick, with happy faces. I always see people like them on the Internet. They live in a different world, one very far from here!"

"What about the other movie?" the fairy asked gently.

"I watch the other one every day," Odi said. "What do you want from me?"

"Odi, please answer a simple question. Which movie did you prefer?"

"Are you kidding me? You already know. It's so obvious. The first movie is about a life of normal people, far away from here, but that's not for me! I'm a freak. I live in a shit hole, hated by my mother, abandoned by my father, abused by my stepfather, and bullied by my brother and a bunch of other morons. The fighting is nonstop. The future for weirdos like me is clear. I was born by mistake! Every day I try to forget that while I fight to survive! So there is no way out, got it? Got it?"

Odi stopped shouting to catch his breath. He was

almost choking from lack of air. He looked at the fairy with tear-filled eyes. "I've always been insignificant. Always! Bastards created me to become one. And my only task is to survive them. I need to gain the upper hand for them to leave me alone. I am nobody and nothing. Why are you bothering me with those glamourous people in the movie? To put me down? Hah! I am already at the bottom! You want to remind me how insignificant, worthless, and fallen I am, don't you?"

Odi was losing his voice. The fairy sat motionlessly, and the little boy looked up at him. Odi was shivering, and the room was spinning. His tears turned into a growing rage he couldn't stop. He'd lost. He was captured by hopelessness, resentment, hatred, and anger. His face turned red. Something picked him up. Some powerful wave of rage grabbed him. He let it seize him. He grabbed a chair, intending to smash something with it. He swung and threw it at the window.

The fairy stepped forward and raised her hand. The chair hovered in mid-air, then gracefully landed behind the table where it belonged.

Odi couldn't believe his eyes. This was too much, way too much. *It's time to split*, Odi thought. He bolted to the door and jerked at the knob several times, but it wouldn't open. Then he ran back, jumped over the counter, and grabbed a knife. "Open the door, witch!" Odi shouted, pointing the blade at her.

The fairy waved her hand again, and the knife slipped out of Odi's hand and back into its original spot.

He started to grab for it again.

Chapter 13

"**N**o! Odi, please stop!" The fairy made soothing hand gestures in the air. "Please, calm down; I understand your pain," she said. "The time has come for you to know everything is alright with you, that you are a good, normal boy."

Odi's eyes shifted from left to right like a cornered animal planning its escape.

"Odi, please look at me," said the fairy.

Odi remained silent, looking from the fairy to the little boy, then back at the fairy again. His vision grew blurry; he'd held his breath for too long. He inhaled deeply and, raising his voice, yelled, "What are you talking about? Do you mean to tell me that good, normal boys have a life like that? Something was wrong with me from the very minute I arrived in this world. I don't even understand why the hell I was even born. My father left me. My mother is always either drunk or depressed. She blames my brother and me for her life of misery with that abusive jerk she married. She said our father left because we were a pain in the butt, were too much work and stress, and she couldn't find a decent man again because of us! So I grew up feeling unwanted and unloved, feeling guilty for my own existence." His eyes glittered with tears, but he held them back.

The fairy's eyes also glittered with tears for his pain. "I know. I feel for you. You came into this world as a tiny angel looking for and expecting love. Instead, you experienced a lack of love, warmth, and caring. Instead, you only felt abandonment, rejection, and cruelty from your parents. Later, you were bullied by your brother."

Suppressed tears from so many years of anguish and sorrow ran down Odi's cheeks.

"You were a mistreated little boy," the fairy continued. "You were confused, frustrated, and scared. As a result, you were traumatized. Finally, like any young child in this situation, you decided something was wrong with you, that you were the cause of all your troubles. You had no choice but to start defending yourself, fight back if you could—or run. You decided then that the world was cruel and dangerous, full of pain, evil, and deception because that was what you saw.

As a little one, you came to these conclusions based on experience," the fairy said, pointing to little Odi, who sat huddled in a chair with tear-filled eyes.

"But now it's time to know, Odi, that there is absolutely nothing wrong with you. You are a good, ordinary boy who's been badly hurt—physically and mentally. But you're better than them and have a stronger will. If you're willing to try, you can find an extraordinary mission to fulfill in life."

That got Odi's attention. He'd cooled down some but still stood clutching the back of the chair, breathing heavily. His face had an expression of bitterness and pain.

The fairy continued, "You need to understand that everyone has a reason for coming into this world. Every single soul has a purpose, task, and mission. No exceptions. And everyone is responsible for fulfilling their purpose."

Odi's eyes glazed over, remembering brutal episodes from his life, one after another. Finally, he raised tear-battled eyes to her. "Why does everyone treat me like garbage?"

The fairy pointed at the younger Odi. "Odi, please, look at this boy. What do you think is wrong with him?"

Odi looked at the little kid. His eyes and whole face switched to empathy. He was searching for the right words to say, looking into the innocent eyes of his little self. He felt a knot in his throat. Who could find it in their heart to hurt such a little angel? He plopped down on the chair next to the table and covered his face with his hands.

The fairy rested her hand on his shoulder. "Odi, listen to me. Nothing since the day you were born has ever been your fault. Unfortunately, in most cases, abused children become adults with a traumatized psychic. Therefore, children who were abused or were hurt in their past grow up and start hurting others. You need to understand that." She gave his shoulder a friendly pat. "Here, I will show you. Give me the flashlight, please."

Odi pulled it out of his pocket and handed it to her. She walked back to the wall, where they'd watched the other two movies. She turned on the flashlight and pointed it at the wall. The movie showed the events of that morning when he'd met the first kid and was running with him from the angry and drunk neighbor.

"Look, Odi, you saved the inner child of your next-door neighbor, the guy who has bullied you all your life. You sensed his suffering. You realized there was nothing terrible about that child, either. It was a crying baby, sitting in a gray box inside an angry adult.

Do you know a child is crying and suffering inside *every* angry, mean, and cruel adult? Everyone who needs to hurt others was damaged as a child—a child who was hurt badly. So you see, it has nothing to do with you. Nothing was your fault then. Nothing is your fault now. You were born an innocent angel and arrived here for a reason and purpose.

Look at me, Odi, she said. All children are angels when they are born: you, your stepfather, your mom, your brother, the neighbor, and all the rest. Unfortunately, the adults traumatized the little angels with their actions, turning these little children into bitter adults, full of anger, aggression, and resentment. Then they carry and spread it into the world. You were given a unique chance to see the crying children sitting in a box inside each of those adults. That is the true gift. To see and understand."

Odi jumped out of his chair. "Yes, the boxes!" I saw the boxes. It was inside them. They all have those boxes. What are they for?"

The fairy smiled slightly, seeing Odi's healing process begin to take shape.

Chapter 14

The fairy brought a tray with steaming hot tea and sat down. "The box is the protective shell an inner child crawls into to survive traumatic events. The walls of these boxes are made of anger, resentment, hatred, revenge, fear, sorrow, disgust, blame, shame, confusion, frustration, anxiety, vulnerability, and guilt. All these emotions and feelings created the gray walls of the boxes they're trapped in. It protects them initially, but later that same box becomes a jail that prevents them from taking all the right paths.

They grow up certain that the world is a dark, evil place and all people are bad, just because they can see nothing but the gray walls from within their box. They look at life through these walls and grow up carrying out the beliefs they were raised with—anger, violence, cruelty, betrayal, hate or shame, disrespect, and blame themselves and others. They don't believe in a different world outside the walls of their box. As long as they are stuck, they will never be able to see that a different reality exists, or if they realize it's even there, they cannot get it. Their dream life will never be realized as long as those walls are up. So while the inner child is in the box—the adult is suffering from limitations.

So, joy, peace, happiness, satisfaction, lightness, optimism, luck, miracles, amazing surprises, and trust in this world is behind the walls. With those built-up negative emotions, it is impossible to have a happy life full of miracles and opportunities."

Odi grew thoughtful. "So, all I need to do is get out of the box, and a new world like the one in the movie will become accessible to me? Is that what you mean?"

The fairy patted Odi's hand. "All one needs to do is make a *choice*, my friend. So which movie did you end up choosing?"

Odi rolled his eyes. "Any fool would choose the first movie, although it's a lie." He said, frowning at the fairy.

The fairy smiled. "Having security, significance, understanding, certainty, growth, acceptance, love, and connection to others are basic human needs. Every baby in this world is an innocent angel, full of the desire to live, who needs love, understanding, acceptance, care, and tenderness. When those angels are bullied or harmed by their loved ones, they develop a defense mechanism.

The key to unlocking it is to choose ... to continue living in the nightmare you've been in all your life or choose to live a different life that is colorful, exciting, and full of love. Of course, life always brings some pain, but *suffering is a choice*. And as you saw in the first movie, a life filled with happiness, laughter, love, and abundance is also your choice."

Odi was about to contradict her but kept silent as she continued.

"It's all about choices you make as you create the life you want. That first movie is about how your future *can* look," she said, emphasizing each word. "You can be that person, the engineer with a happy family and a beautiful, healthy, wealthy life. We all have different scenarios of what our lives can become. Every scenario develops according to the choices you make today.

If you wish to have a chance at opportunities and accomplish the great things destined in your new life, you must abandon the dark path of anger, revenge, resentment, hatred, violence, shame, and blame to others and yourself. The choices you made yesterday shaped your life until today. Your choices now, today, and tomorrow, will determine your destiny. Now that you know all of that, you'll be better able to start on your recovery journey. So, renounce all those bad negative feelings—for good! They are not benefiting you in any way."

The fairy pushed her cup aside. "Your angel tested you with the first little boy, the inner child of your nemesis, your neighbor. And you rescued him. You got it done. Therefore, you were entrusted with the flashlight. All of the aids given to you were designed to provide you with a chance to see how things work."

Odi looked at his little self. The kid was still sitting at the table, his eyes glistening with tears. He felt the pain of his little Odi … he felt pain for himself.

Chapter 15

"**Y**our other option is the second movie. It is your destiny if you choose to remain the same. But you need to know something about the second movie."

Odi gazed into the calming eyes of the fairy. "What else is there to know? Everything seems pretty clear to me," Odi replied, his face expressing disdain and pain.

"Odi, that is your destiny right now. If nothing is done to change it, you will remain right there," the fairy said, her eyes piercing into his.

Odi felt as if he were losing the battle. Everything was turning upside down. Trying to hide his feelings, he replied, "No, no, no … how is that possible? I am nothing like them! I was even going to run away soon."

The fairy looked at him with compassion and sighed deeply. "My friend, you are already at the threshold of this path. Do you remember your thoughts this morning and every other morning? You hate your enemies and dream of making them all pay before you run away. I feel your pain, Odi; I do. But you've already developed defense mechanisms to ease the traumas you've been exposed to since you were a baby.

Unfortunately, now these mechanisms own you and control your life, making you repeat your mom's and stepfather's patterns. So even if you think you'll never be like them, you will."

At the negative shake of Odi's head, she said, "Try to understand, Odi. As unfortunate as it is, you're stuck in the same box as the other children you saw by not letting yourself see a different world and different people."

"My parents didn't love me, and my stepfather beat the shit out of me since I was a little kid. How can I..?"

"Yes, yes, all of that happened. But it is totally up to you now on what you choose," interrupted the fairy. "You choose to hate everybody, and unfortunately, in your current life, there is no one else but you. But what if there was something else possible for you? Another path to take, and you're in control of making the decisions to get you there?"

Odi stayed quiet for a minute, processing what he'd just learned. He could hear his heartbeat in his ears, pounding like a huge clock ticking out time. Finally, when he felt his breathing calm, he said, "If I let go of revenge, I will become weak! Anyone can knock me down! What are my chances of escaping it? How can I even get into college to get a chance to become an inventor? It's all just a fairy tale!"

"Don't worry about the how's right now, Odi," the fairy replied. "You're still sitting in a gray box, without the slightest idea of what opportunities lay ahead for you, even in theory, and there may be supporters to help you.

You choose instead to concern yourself with all you will lose. What you will lose has everything to do with what you will gain. It's not your responsibility or your job to figure out the how yet. But once you choose to change, the universe will shift things around to make that happen. Your job is to get out of the box—completely and permanently! If you do, I promise you a new reality where you can envision your opportunities, which will be a whole different universe!"

The fairy raised her hands to the heavens. "But," her voice thundered. *But—but—but—but echoed from somewhere.* "To get out of the box, you must leave behind the path of anger, revenge, and violence." *Vengeance, violence—violence—violence*—echoed again. "You worry about being powerless. On the contrary, it is a sign of tremendous strength, not weakness," the fairy said, pausing after each word, so they echoed again.

"That kind of wisdom gives you immense power and opens new doors to release many new opportunities. But retreating to hate, fear, fury, and resentment—hiding in a box—is the true weakness," she said.

"There is another truth you need to know. The ability to empathize with another's pain and show compassion for the inner child of an offender *is* showing your power. The box full of disruptive feelings was created to defend a traumatized child's mind. Holding on to those negative feelings and deep beliefs about yourself signifies total defeat. It is a child's way of thinking. Every time you put yourself into your box, it is the behavior of an offended child. Look at me, Odi," the fairy said with a smile. "Always remember that!"

Abruptly little Odi screamed. "Odi! Odi! I feel like we are in danger right now!"

Suddenly, Odi felt something heavy land on his head.

Boom!

Chapter 16

O di was three years old again. He was not at the daycare and couldn't remember why. It was only him and his stepfather at home. Sam had been drinking beer all day and was now watching basketball on TV.

Odi was bored and wanted to play. His birth father had played mini foosball with him, and he'd liked it so much. So Odi brought the heavy foosball board game over to his stepfather to play. He stretched out his little arms, saying, "play."

"Get away from me!" shouted his stepfather. Then, snatching the game from the boy's hands, he threw it on the floor.

Little Odi's lips began to tremble. His eyes filled with tears and rained down his cheeks. Then, pulling himself together, he picked up the game and handed it to his stepfather again.

This time his stepfather got very angry. "Are you dumb? Don't bother me!" he hissed. He grabbed the game and bashed little Odi with it, using all his might. The blow knocked the boy off his feet. He fell on his back, hitting his head on the floor.

Big Odi's heart sank as he remembered the immense pain in the back of his head that day. He rushed forward and stepped inside the image to help little Odi. He lifted the sobbing boy from the floor and pressed him tightly to his chest. He closed his eyes, full of tears, hugging him as he'd wanted to be embraced all these years.

With one hand, he rubbed the back of little Odi's head, trying to relieve some of the intense pain from his fall. He remembered this scene very well and the acute pain he'd experienced for one so young.

Little Odi wept uncontrollably from the pain and despair.

"Shh, shh, little one," Odi said, swaying with him. "You are safe now. He will never hurt you again while I'm here. You are not alone anymore. I will protect you. Shh, Shh."

His stepfather's voice boomed out from behind him. "Who the hell are you? What are you doing in my apartment?"

His stepfather's voice echoed in big Odi's head. "And we're back," Odi said. His eyes flashed like two beacons of lights through the darkness aimed at his stepfather. "Your apartment? You are a parasitic snake who slithered in here on your belly one day, abusing a lost woman and helpless little kids." Odi gave him a dismissive quirk with his chin. "Hell, I'm surprised you don't hiss when you speak," he said, surprised at himself.

"What???" His stepfather's eyes narrowed with rage, and he jerked his fists up at Odi and the kid. Odi pulled himself up to his full height and pushed little Odi behind him as he prepared to fight.

Suddenly, the golden feather escaped from his pocket. His stepfather froze mid-step with an evil grimace on his face and clenched fists.

Odi remembered the magic flashlight and quickly grabbed it from his back pocket. He saw the scared, crying boy inside his stepfather's box. His anger let go of him instantly. His chest felt tight, and he was overwhelmed by emotions. The hate for his stepfather was mixed with compassion for the sad, crying child inside him.

He looked at little Odi beside him, still wiping away his tears with the back of his hand. He felt so sorry for him. Looking at this frustrated, helpless, and hopeless child (himself), his anger rolled over to the one who had offended and hurt him so badly. He started to fill with rage again.

Odi's eyes filled with tears. He felt sorry for his little self, and it would be easy to pour his hatred out onto the offender (his stepfather) and vent his feelings by expressing aggression. He most certainly would have done that yesterday. Hell, he'd already done that for thirteen years. But now he saw this crying little boy inside his offender, and it pulled on his heart strings. That sad little boy was as scared and hurt as he was.

Odi craved the urge to bring violence to his stepfather and even tried to resist looking into the eyes of the crying child inside the box. His brain tried to process it all to create an adverse reaction, but before he could fully conjure it, he was interrupted by the voice of little Odi.

"Baby ... baby, cry," he said, pointing to the little child inside their stepfather, frozen by the angel's feather.

Odi looked at little Odi with adoration. Little kids were pure angels. "Yes. There is a crying baby, even inside this asshole," Odi said in a very adult manner, full of understanding.

His stepfather had offended, beaten, and mocked him for ten years. Finally, he'd gotten used to hating him. He dreamed of revenge every morning, noon, and night, but the new information he'd learned from the fairy now entered into the equation, withholding the ossified habitual feelings and emotions he used to have.

It felt like a dam had burst within him, and after seeing this unfortunate, sobbing, and tormented child inside his stepfather, he knew he couldn't act and feel the same way he used to. So he pulled himself together and approached the inner child of his stepfather. "Hey, kid, how are you doing? Not so good, right?"

The child inside his stepfather stopped crying and stared at him with big, tear-stained eyes.

"Would you like to get rid of that yucky box you're in?" asked Odi, holding his hands out to him. "Don't be scared, little one. I think I can help you."

The boy held tightly onto the sides of his box.

Odi tried another tactic. "You know this box is a dangerous place. It makes you and your adult suffer, and it makes him very cruel. He is angry and hurts others because you are sitting inside this box. You are not well in there; can you not see?"

The kid looked at Odi with the mistrust and fear of a wounded animal.

Odi tried again. "Look at me, I'm not angry, and I am not yelling at or hurting you. Look, this is my inner child, little Odi. He's just like you."

His stepfather's inner child looked little Odi over for a few minutes, then back at big Odi.

Odi held his hand out to the little boy. "Come on. Let me help you," he coaxed. "You're going to feel much better without this horrible box,"

The boy slowly and reluctantly extended his tiny hand

Odi had mixed feelings, seeing the sweet inner child in front of him, knowing it was the same monster he'd thought of killing just that morning. He trembled at the thought while looking into the crystal-clear eyes of the child, who was about to touch his hand. He felt that familiar knot in his throat again, trying to hold back tears.

He hated tears. He hated weakness.

Then he heard the same familiar, soft, piercing voice of the fairy in his head, words he'd just listened to a few minutes ago in the coffee shop. *"If you wish to receive new opportunities and achieve great things in life, you must eliminate the anger, resentment, hate, violence, and hostility inside you. Get rid of that ugly box that made those feelings. Get rid of it for good. It is the only way."*

Odi surrendered. For the first time in his life, he'd relinquished his fear of something new and unfamiliar, yet it felt—great! There was no other word to describe it. He didn't quite understand what was happening, but something bright and wonderful had expanded in his chest.

He looked at his stepfather's inner child in the box with compassion and kindness, then reached for his hand. As soon as they touched, the child vanished, and Odi and little Odi were back in the coffee shop again.

Chapter 17

O di understood that something incredible had just happened. He'd made a big, conscious, and mature choice. The right choice. He'd learned from past experiences to be very cautious, or the world would beat him down. Now he laughed at his naiveté.

"Well, there we are," the fairy said with a chuckle. She knew it was time to help set him free.

Odi looked at his inner child. The little one was smiling, looking back and forth between the fairy and Odi as if he were waiting for them to do something.

The fairy broke the awkward silence. "Odi … please … go over to this little you and give him a big hug. Give him all the love, support, and compassion he didn't get from the others. He didn't have a loving mother and father to hug him with love, but he has *you*. Go to him now, please," the fairy pleaded. "Go to yourself and give your all to him to help you heal. It's never too late to give love and support to your inner child … to yourself," she said softly.

Tears flowed freely from Odi's eyes, and he could

hold them back any longer. He rushed towards the little Odi and hugged him as tightly as he had always dreamed of being hugged by someone who loved him.

He howled like a wounded dog relieving his tormented soul. As Odi relinquished his anguish, agony, and all the pain of his bodily injuries in his short 13 years, he no longer felt disgraced, even by his tears.

Odi squeezed his little self in his arms, stroking his head. Hot tears streamed down his cheeks into the little one's hair.

Little Odi snuggled toward him and tightly closed his eyes. He also cried. It was an act of great liberation from all the grief that he had experienced.

It lasted 15 minutes. The fairy stood in silence, not wanting to break the spell. Her eyes also glittered with tears. It seemed the whole world had stopped letting these two youngsters cry out all the pain and anguish in their souls.

Big Odi got down on one knee and put his hands on little Odi's shoulders. "I love you, kid. I love you," he groaned. "Now that I know about you, I'll give you all the love I never had. I'm old enough to take care of us now, and we'll make it, I promise."

Odi looked down at his belly. Even without a flashlight, he could see a large crack in his gray box.

Little Odi gave him a toothy smile, stepped back into the box, and disappeared. Big Odi froze in amazement.

The smooth, familiar, melodic voice behind him interrupted his train of thought. "I knew you could do it!"

Odi turned around to find his guardian angel, as always, leaning against a wall.

The angel nudged the fairy. "You see, I told you he is special."

The fairy shook her head with an approving nod.

"By the way, Odi, the angel said," by allowing yourself to console your inner child like a superhero, you can give him all the love that he never received—that *you* did not receive. It is how you can get through your most difficult memories and help protect yourself. With this system, you will help heal yourself and your inner child."

Odi remained quiet. He stood up and tried to pull himself together. This day had been very draining. He looked out the window. The sun peeked through the clouds.

There was a sudden knock at the door of the coffee shop. The fairy looked up and frowned, "Since when do you ever knock, elf?"

Chapter 18

T he door opened, and an elf entered. He wore a small, intricate silk green jacket, pants, and a strange little green hat.

The fairy frowned. "Long time no see, elf. How can I help you?"

"What? Don't you remember our conversation?" Standing in the doorway, he looked around the coffee shop, paused for a second or two on Odi, then turned to the fairy again. "I need a helper!" he said, throwing his hands in the air.

Odi observed their unfriendly banter and wondered what was going on. He looked around for the angel, but he seemed to have vanished again.

"Why would Santa's helper need a helper?" the fairy asked sarcastically.

The elf hopped up on the bar so she could see him better. "You have no helpers at all," he countered. "Who would work with such a grouch!" the elf grunted.

The fairy gave him 'the look.'

The elf cleared his throat. He'd overstepped his

boundaries. "Well, Madam," he said humbly, "I need a helper, or else I won't be able to get everything ready for Christmas, and there goes my promotion. You know what my boss is like."

"It's half a year until Christmas," the fairy said, wiping the bar recently vacated by a patron.

"Exactly! Only half a year away," cried the elf.

The fairy glanced at Odi and lowered her voice to the elf. "This is not the right time to discuss looking for a helper. We are in the middle of a crisis here."

Odi's heart started beating rapidly, and his thoughts went wild. *Santa's helper? Really? Really?* Then he switched. "You are all screwed up here! Santa doesn't exist. That's only crap they feed little kids in fairy tales, so they'll behave once a year!"

The fairy and elf glared at him, turned away, and kept talking.

The fairy looked thoughtful. "And what would this helper need to do?"

"Yes, I'd also like to know," Odi sarcastically.

The elf looked Odi up and down. "Who's the kid," he asked the fairy.

"That's Odi," she said.

The elf pivoted from the fairy to Odi and back. "Oh, well, that explains everything." Then, at Odi's glaring look, he said, "what skills do you have, boy?"

Odi decided to play along. "Oh, many. Why I can do anything! I'm a good runner and fighter, and I have recently developed a huge sense of humor," he said sarcastically.

The elf gave a dismissive wave with his hand. "Nah, boy, you won't need to fight. Here's what I need." He shoved a list in front of Odi. "I need a second person to fly around the cities, count the children getting presents, and take notes of what presents to get. Then, of course, we get their letters, but if something gets mixed up, I get penalized."

Odi blinked. "Are you being serious right now?"

"Of course, I am," the elf said. *Was the boy cracked in his head?*

The fairy laughed. "Odi, you did say you dreamt of traveling, right?"

"Yes, I did ... but ... ." Odi replied, still confused. Of course, he'd dreamt of it—he wanted it more than anything!

The fairy smiled. "Then why wait? Everything is possible right now."

The elf grew impatient. "Are you interested in this job or not, boy?"

Odi swung around in his chair to face the tiny elf. "Job? Are you for real? I mean, you're not joking, right?"

The elf stamped his tiny foot. "Of course, my offer is for real! Are you going to go or not? I don't have any more time to waste," the elf snapped.

Odi jumped out of his chair in a flash. "Yes, I'm interested. It was just unexpected! Does Santa really exist?"

The elf turned to the fairy. "Where did you find him?" he said, pointing his thumb over his shoulder at Odi.

Odi didn't want to miss this opportunity. It would give him the money he needed to leave his home forever. Finally, the wonders the fairy had told him from the beginning were coming true! "Yes, I am ready! When do we fly—and how?"

"Oh no, not that; Odi is not ready to fly yet!" The fairy objected.

"Madam, I'm out of time," the elf hissed. "I already told you, I only have half a year left." He turned to Odi and asked, "Are you ready, boy?"

Chapter 19

"**Y**ou bet I am!" Odi looked left and right. "Right now?"

"No, in a year … of course, right now!" the elf said with unexpected kindness. He had sensed Odi's enthusiasm. He snapped his fingers, and something humongous landed outside the window on the street. It sparkled in the sunlight outside the windows.

"Was that Santa's sleigh?" Odi wondered.

The fairy drew in a sharp breath. "Oh my goodness, it's that big galoot again, isn't it!" She shook her fist at the elf. "If he breaks my window like last time, you will pay for the repairs!" she yelled to the elf, who was already walking to the entrance with Odi.

Odi barely noticed the fairy yelling after them as he followed the elf outside. For some reason, the street was empty, but why? Then, he heard a loud snort and looked up. The answer stood right in front of the coffee shop. It was the most gigantic, most magnificent creature Odi had ever seen! It had the body, hind legs, and tail of a lion, but it had the head and wings of an eagle. The animal was staring right at him with its big, emerald, green eyes.

"Wow! That's so dope!" Odi said, astonished. "Is it some kind of dragon?"

"Oh, no! It's a griffin," the elf replied.

"Gri ... what?" Odi was trying to repeat the word.

"Griffin," the elf pronounced the name again loud and clear.

"That's what I thought you said." Odi tipped his head in confusion. "What is a griffin?" He'd heard all about dragons but never about griffins.

"Yes, yes, a griffin." The elf checked the animal's colossal harness. "He's just a huge, hungry animal, constantly messing up my work, aren't you, boy?" he affectionally patted the griffin's massive head. "Why, he can't even fly ten miles without landing to eat something!"

Odi burst into laughter. It felt good. "What does he eat, I wonder?"

"He eats fish. Only fish and a ton of it at best!"

The elf moved in front of the griffin.

The griffin bowed his massive eagle head before the elf, waiting for him to put his bridle on. The elf gently caressed his head, and the creature purred like a kitten in satisfaction, closing his emerald eyes halfway.

The elf turned to Odi. "So, my friend, are you ready to take the flight of a lifetime?"

Odi looked horrified. "A flight ... on him ... alone?"

"Yes, but don't worry. You two can practice to-gether." The elf and the griffin exchanged a look, and Odie swore he heard the beast chuckle.

"Don't worry. You'll get the hang of flying him. It's easy, just like flying a small plane. Here, let me show you." The elf hopped up behind the griffin's enormous neck. "You'll need to sit close to his head. When you pull his feathers to the right, he'll go right, and to the left, he'll go left. Pull up—he goes higher, down—lower. Oh, and don't be afraid to slide off of him. If you do, he'll scoop you up right away. He's been trained for that, right boy?" The elf gently ruffled the feathers on the griffin's head.

Odi's knees got weak, and he thought he might throw up. What had he signed up for? He'd be lucky to stay alive after this kind of flight, and without safety belts, a parachute, or anything else, it seemed inevitable. But it was too late to back out now. *I must do what I must do.* So he climbed up on top of the griffin, who stood completely still for him as a sign of affection.

Chapter 20

The elf handed Odi the reins. "Be on your way, guys!" He pointed to a brown satchel under the griffin's neck feathers. The notebooks are in there, with the instructions, so take a look on your way. The griffin knows the route." The elf pulled an antique watch on a chain out of his pocket and checked the time. "Oh, my, you need to hurry up and go!"

Odi didn't have a chance to answer. He hardly managed to pet the feathers on the griffin's neck before the animal spread his massive wings and took off at a gallop. Never in his life had Odi screamed so loudly. Saying he was terrified didn't even begin to describe it. His heart was pounding! The wind was blasting him in his face taking his breath away.

He tried to catch his breath and stay balanced. The griffin, obviously enjoying the newbie's reaction, showed off by making large, intricate circles in the sky, using Odi's unintentional commands.

Odi quickly figured out that any accidental jerk on the griffin's feathers made him change directions, and since the practice was the fastest way to learn, 15-minutes later, Odi was in complete control of the beast.

Together, they looped in and around small towns. Soon, the griffin began to fly lower, looking for a place to land. It was then that Odi noticed some commotion below. It was getting dark anyway, so they might as well land. He signaled the griffin to go down, and they settled on a house rooftop. No one had noticed them yet.

Below, they witnessed a shocking scene. A boy was standing with his head bowed in front of a bunch of children and their parents. His parents were humiliating their son in front of everyone.

"You are an embarrassment to our family, Pit! Let everyone see and know what a piece of shit you are," his mother yelled.

Pit's father cuffed the boy on the side of his head. "I don't know why we've been supporting this dummy."

Pit's ear was already swelling. He was so humiliated he wanted to die. He tried to hold back his tears, but he couldn't take the pain any longer, so he cried.

"Oh, there ya go," his father said. "Shut up, ya crybaby, or I'll blast you again!"

His mother came and knelt beside him. "You are a useless, worthless child who is always in the way of my happiness," his mother hissed in her child's ear, adding, "I'm sorry I didn't have an abortion!"

She yanked him by his arm and dragged him to the ground by the people's feet. "Now, be more grateful for your life and stop embarrassing me in front of these decent people!" She yanked Pitt back on his feet. "Apologize this instant for that smashed window now, in front of everyone!" she said through clenched teeth.

His classmates howled with laughter at him. Their parents whispered amongst themselves, but they didn't intervene.

Odi quickly hopped off the griffin. He'd witnessed most of the strange and horrid spectacle. Murder rose in his mind as he wildly searched for stairs to get down. He quickly located the fire escape and ran down it. Then, with fists clenched, he went running toward the crowd. "You are all going to regret you were ever born!"

Odi searched for a big rock, and when he found one, he yelled into the crowd, "Hey, all of you! Get away from him! Look at what you're doing to him! Do you realize how he feels right now? Back off! I have enough rocks here for all of you!"

Odi looked up for the Griffin, but he was gone. *Oh boy, now I'm alone without a backup*, Odi realized. He mechanically pulled the flashlight from his pocket to see in the dark.

Chapter 21

O di was so mad that he nearly hurdled the first rock at the boy's father until the flashlight's beam illuminated him. He saw the same familiar, ugly gray box with a miserable child inside.

It was the same with Pit's mom. Her inner child was sobbing loudly inside of her.

Odi looked into the crowd of adults. Each had a gray box inside, holding their inner child hostage. They were all scared to death and upset about what was happening. Everyone's story was painfully clear. It was shown as a movie from an old projector— beatings, humiliation, insults, verbal abuse, disregard, lack of love, callousness, criticism, and barbarity from none other than those closest to them—their parents—the people they trusted.

As Odi observed them, he shook violently from head to toe. He bit his lower so hard to keep it from trembling that he tasted blood. Gigantic tears gathered in his eyes, but he refused to shed them. They were tears of horror, pain, anger, and disappointment for the parents and sadness for their children.

It was tearing at his soul.

The adult crowd robotically turned to Odi. The big rock fell out of Odi's hand, making a dull thud on the pavement. *I can't do it.* He reached out for the golden feather in his pocket. Waving the feather, he made time stand still.

Odi didn't notice, but the angel was leaning against the wall, observing him. The griffin was there as well—he'd never really left; he'd just grabbed a quick bite to eat.

Everyone remained in a surreal state, staring blankly at Odi. Then, a tiny fire ignited in his heart. It started growing and turned warm and bright like a kiss from the sun. It filled his chest, and golden rays beamed beyond his body. The sun beams illuminated his surroundings, extending towards the sobbing kids.

For the first time in his life, Odi felt genuine empathy. And it felt so good. The angel witnessed what Odi hadn't—a miracle. He was too busy.

As soon as Odi stopped time and made everything in the universe stand still, he went over to the little children. "Hi, kids! I'm Odi. How are you doing? Not so good, right? Let's calm down and see what we can do here," he told them.

He didn't know he was being observed. He just wanted to help the little ones. He already knew how important it was.

Odi remembered he had a bunch of napkins in his pocket. Now it all made sense. He took the napkins out and started wiping away the children's tears. "Now, listen to me carefully. You must throw away your boxes if you want to get rid of the stink for good." Finally, the children started to calm down and stared at him.

"One more time, boys, and girls. Now, pay attention," Odi said sternly. "If you wish to be like the ones who beat and humiliate you, stay inside those creepy boxes. But if you choose not to be contaminated by aggression and oppression, you must first eliminate it. If you don't wish to be terrifying monsters instilling fear in your children someday, throw away your boxes. No one can do it for you. Oh, and one more thing, you are not as helpless as you think!"

He didn't know whether they believed him or not.

The children remained silent. Odi didn't know what to do next. His energy spent, he just stood there, quietly looking at the kids and their frozen parents.

Suddenly, time started ticking again—everything came back to life—and everyone. At first, they looked at each other dazed and confused, as if they had no idea what they were doing there. Then, all of a sudden, the inner child of Pit's father threw his box on the ground. It turned to dust. Then, all the other parents, amazed by Odi's speech, threw their boxes on the ground, and everyone else followed.

Odi took a deep breath. He saw the angel in the distance giving him the thumbs-up. Odi approached the inner child of the boy's mother (Pit was silent, looking at Odi with admiration) and gently stroked her hair. She smiled.

Odi celebrated all the way to his soul, and for now, he had the griffin to help him see from high above all the injustice within his reach. And he would reach out to them all. A strong headwind whipped through the trees. Odi and the griffin were ready to go!

Chapter 22

Upon landing, Odi heard the elf shouting his name. He turned and saw him waving wildly at them.

The griffin gave what looked like a smile to Odi and wiggled his tail in a friendly manner. Odi jumped off the griffin and ran over to meet him.

The elf gave Odi a hearty slap on his back. "Great job, boy. I'm so proud of you!"

Odi beamed at that. No one had ever given him a compliment in his entire life!

The elf wiggled his eyebrows. "So, are you ready to work with us again?" he asked cheerfully.

"Boy, am I!" Odi hopped back onto the griffin's back and gave him a pat on his massive neck. Deep inside, where his inner child still lived, he felt happy and fulfilled. For the first time in his life, he was surrounded by the support and care he desperately needed. Now he knew they were always around, watching out after him. For the first time ever, he didn't feel lonely. Instead, he felt wanted, needed, protected, and significant.

The griffin spread his magnificent wings and sped off with Odi riding high on his back.

They floated between the clouds. When Odi looked down, he noticed the houses were gray. The roads, the cars, and the river lined with boats were gray. Everything seemed to be shrouded in a gray smog.

Odi grew thoughtful for a moment. *Could the world that the fairy had shown him exist within this type of reality? He smiled. Dude, what are you thinking? Of course, it can! Look at you right now. You're riding a beautiful griffin and helping an elf who works for Santa! This is happening right now ... so everything is possible!*

Odi and the griffin drifted in and out of the clean, white puffy clouds. He started to say something in the griffin's ear about the gray world beneath his wings when he noticed something bright and colorful on the horizon.

Odi directed the griffin towards it. With a tight grip on his neck feathers, he sat straight as the wind increased. A few minutes later, they found themselves flying over a beautiful meadow of flowers. Odi was dazed. He'd never seen such an abundance of beauty and colors—not even in movies or social media. It was a vibrant, luminous sea of how life could be. It smelled different here—clean and fresh—and music and laughter were coming from below.

Odi's old world had suddenly turned into a big gray dot that kept getting smaller and smaller.

He observed the towns they flew over. Some were bigger than his; others were smaller—almost like villages. Life was in full swing everywhere.

As the griffin slowly circled above town after town, Odi could see people and how they lived. There were huge mansions and quaint homes, large crowds, and smaller groups, but most importantly, Odi's open, the sensitive heart could tell at first glance that most of the families were happy. That most of the children were nurtured by their parents. His heart ached.

Odi asked the griffin to make several rounds over some of the areas while he looked into everyone's eyes repeatedly. By afternoon, they'd visited so many places he'd lost track of time. Still, eventually, he remembered the elf's assignment and started counting, writing down information about all the kids and their Christmas wishes. He'd never felt so valuable before.

He'd observed thousands of families. The children were happy and joyfully playing—even in poor neighborhoods; they didn't have a lot of things, but they were loved and cared for by their parents.

He also noticed lonely kids, feeling unloved by their parents—abused, miserable, scared, lonely kids in beautiful, lavish homes, surrounded by the best toys money could buy, which they had no interest in playing with.

Some of these kids dreamed of receiving their mom's and dad's attention and affection. Many even wanted that for Christmas, while others wished for another expensive toy to hopefully relieve their pain.

Odi couldn't understand why some low-income families could have so much love and joy in their lives and how families who seemingly had everything they wished for could be so miserable. But, the more homes he visited, the clearer it became.

He compiled his data and concluded that the most essential thing in life wanted by every child was to be loved, protected, respected, and needed. Bliss for them meant having their parents' attention and spending time together. The best games were the ones played with their mom and dad.

It touched his heart. He wondered, *what does Santa* give *the kids who don't wish for toys but have wishes like, "I want my mom and dad to play with me?"*

Chapter 23

Once again, Odi's soul was filled with empathy. He felt sorry for those kids. He'd been a kid like that, too.

He could see now which kids had started to build that filthy, stinking gray box around them. But unfortunately, he wasn't physically able to help them all. So he could only send everyone a ray of light, hope, and compassion.

When they finally reached the last town on the list, Odi realized he was hungry. He found some coins in his pocket, which he figured would be enough for a hotdog or hamburger. He didn't feel like stealing, although he'd often stole chips from a supermarket whenever he'd been hungry. He didn't want to think about his old life right now.

"Hey, griff, could you come in for a landing? I want to get something to eat."

The griffin snorted and slowed down immediately. They landed on the nearby roof of a small building. Odi told the Griffin, "Wait for me here. I'll be back in a jiffy." He headed down the fire escape and ran towards the nearest grocery store.

Chapter 24

Upon entering the grocery store, Odi was dumbfounded. He had no idea food could look so good. Everything was neatly displayed; the fruit and vegetables were perfectly arranged. They almost looked fake because they were so perfect.

Finally, he saw an area where he could sit and enjoy his purchased meal. The prices were insane, and he could only afford the cheapest hamburger. He sat at a table by a window and devoured his meal. A family was seated at a nearby table; two kids and their parents. There was a cart full of groceries next to them. They'd finished their shopping and sat down to have a bite.

The woman and kids were facing away from Odi, and the man was sitting across from him. His features seemed familiar. Odi chewed his burger while observing the man so he wouldn't notice. But the father was too busy talking and joking with his family to see anything else in the world. He was playing around with the children, winking at his wife, and the kids—a boy and a girl—were all smiles and giggles.

" … And then they offered me a great contract,"

the man said, not changing his playful tone of voice, looking into his wife's eyes, clearly waiting for her reaction.

Odi kept staring at his face; sure, he'd seen him somewhere.

The wife hesitated momentarily and exclaimed, "Odi, my love! You did it! I'm so very proud of you!"

Even though her back was to him, Odi could picture her bright smile. The man looked overjoyed, his eyes sparkling with love and delight.

Odi's jaw dropped, and his mouth fell wide open. He caught himself staring and quickly looked away because he'd just realized that the man was him in the future.

That blissful man who'd just shared his happy and exciting news about his new career offer that would affect his most awesome family was Odi!

This man was nothing like the monster Odi had seen in the second movie on the wall of the coffee shop. Odi couldn't even see the man's inner child—little Odi, because he wasn't trapped inside any box.

Odi lingered to take in the incredible aromas so foreign to him. As he sat there, holding on to every moment and inhaling the fragrant smells, he realized he'd finished his meal. He liked it there so much that he didn't want to leave. But then he remembered he was in charge of an important job, one still needed to be completed, so he glanced at everyone one last time and quietly exited the grocery store to return to the griffin.

He felt so happy inside and very confident. He'd seen his future with his own eyes. Not only did he see it, but he had also been close enough to talk to them if he wanted to. He'd felt such an abundance of love and warmth radiating from them that he couldn't wait to meet them someday. He couldn't believe this was happening. His life looked a lot brighter now, and it became clear what he needed to do.

Odi found the building where he'd left the griffin, climbed up to the roof, and found him purring in contentment and licking his enormous paws. Fish heads, fins, and bones were everywhere and smelled very—fishy.

"What a glutton," Odi chuckled as he climbed on top of the animal and patted him on his massive head. They took off soaring into the awaiting, puffy clouds and headed back to the coffee shop. On the way there, Odi realized there were no limits to this bright and colorful world. He knew they hadn't visited every town (clearly, Santa had more than one elf working for him), but what Odi had witnessed today had been genuinely remarkable!

He'd gotten so used to traveling in this beautiful world that the thought of returning to his gave him a weird sense of anxiety. But at the same time, he thought of the children he had rescued. And something warm and fuzzy filled his chest, making him feel better.

It wasn't long before the gray spot on the horizon appeared. It was Odi's old universe. But something had changed ... it seemed to have become lighter. His old-world appeared to have gotten smaller and a bit more trivial.

This time, Odi could see some bright areas here and there against the mostly gray background.

Chapter 25

As they neared the ground, Odi realized what the colorful dots were. They were children. Real kids and the inner children of the adults. While he had been gone, something here had transformed. It felt like early spring, right after a harsh winter, when the first fragile grass and flowers broke through the ground. It was still cloudy here. Odi had no idea how much time had passed, but there was still some daylight.

They landed right next to the coffee shop. The fairy and the elf stood by the entrance to greet them. Odi jumped off the griffin like he'd done it all his life. The griffin nestled his head near Odi's for petting. Odi ruffled the griffin's feathers. "Yes, buddy, you did a great job!" Odi said.

The elf and the fairy ran towards them. "So, Odi," the elf asked impatiently, "how did it go? Did you count everything and write it down?"

Odi held out a notebook with all the data he'd gathered during his trip.

He kept looking at the fairy. Then, reading his

facial expression, she asked, "Did anything happen during the trip that you want to talk about?"

"Yes," Odi replied. "I saw the main character of the first movie you showed me. I sat right across from him—I mean me, and his wife and children were with him!"

"What character?" The elf glanced at the fairy, confused.

She ignored him. "So, you saw yourself in your bright new future option?" the fairy said, smiling. "And what did he … you look like?"

Odi grinned. "He looked happy. Everything was good with him. He was normal … I am normal. He is loved and has a wonderful, happy family he loves and respects." Odi smiled. "He is also very successful because his family works as a team to help support his career. So this is all possible!"

He grabbed the fairy's hands and danced in a circle with her in excitement. "The best day EVER!" he said, twirling her around. "Today, I learned that everything you showed me is possible!" He felt he was about to cry but restrained himself—too many experiences in one day—way too many.

The fairy laughed, and when they stopped dancing, she fanned herself with her handkerchief. "Remember, it's a model of what can be yours if you work hard to get it." She took his hands in hers. "You have been blessed, Odi, with a quick mind and a willingness to change, so more remarkable opportunities will surely come your way."

Odi nodded and said, "you know, it's been awesome spending time with all of you, and I'd love to keep on working." Then, he turned to the elf. "I still need to look for my friend, Dina, but I'll be back soon."

"Certainly, certainly," The fairy said. "Why, I completely forgot about the time."

The elf took his hat off and threw it down on the pavement in front of him. "Is that it?" he exclaimed, looking back and forth between Odi and the fairy. "There's still a ton of work to be done, you know!"

"I told you I'd be back!" Odi assured him.

The fairy turned to Odi. "Wait a minute. On your way home, could you please do me a favor and check up on a customer of mine? I haven't seen her in a while and don't have her number. However, I'll give you her address. You don't have to go in; just yell by her window. She lives on the third floor, and she'll peek out. Tell her the owner of the coffee shop sends her regards.

"Why don't you pay her a visit yourself?" Odi asked.

"I can't leave the shop," the fairy promptly replied and handed him a piece of paper with the address.

Odi hesitated. He'd already spent too much time here and was worried about Dina. But the address was in his neighborhood, and the fairy had done so many amazing things for him that he couldn't refuse.

The fairy produced a steaming cup of hot coffee. She snapped the lid on it. "Here, you're all set. You can give this to her."

Chapter 26

Odi took the cup from her and bid farewell to his new friends. He dragged his feet on his trip to the house of the fairy's customer. He wanted to get it over with quickly and hurry to look for Dina. When he got to the house, he realized that the fairy hadn't given him the name of the lady to call on.

Odi stood in front of the windows and shouted, "Oh miss lady mam, halloo, the coffee shop lady says hi!" Silence. "Hey, who wants some coffee in the neighborhood? Hello?" 10 minutes passed with him getting angrier through every one of them. She wasn't home. More wasted time. Now he was pissed. *What kind of crap was this, anyway?* He needed to find Dina. He threw the cup to the ground in anger.

Suddenly, he noticed a pack of dogs moving up the street towards him, and they didn't look friendly. Their coats were clumpy, and rubbery slobber was dripping from long fangs. Their eyes were bloodshot, and they seemed very strange.

"Where? ... How did they get here?" Odi had heard of stray dogs being caught and taken to the local shelters, but he wasn't aware of packs of dogs wandering loose in his neighborhood.

They moved straight toward him, but when they were just a couple of feet away, Odi realized they weren't dogs … they looked more like—hyenas!

The biggest one, clearly the leader, began to speak, "Well, well, well, Odi, how was your flight?" he asked in a deep, husky whisper.

Odi could smell the stench from the creature's mouth, like the unbearable stink of rotten eggs. He froze in fear while trying hard not to throw up. The street was empty, of course. "Flight? I … I had a great flight … " Odi's eyes darted from that one to the others, following their every move.

The beast kept creeping closer. "Did you see anything exciting?" he asked sarcastically.

"Who are you?" Odi snapped, looking around for some kind of a weapon—a stick, a rock, or whatever else was close.

"Don't bother to look for a way out, Odi," he hissed as if knowing what was running through Odi's mind. "Nothing can help you now since we're already here. Do you think anyone would miss you?" The leader of the herd grinned. "Who do you think you are?"

That did it. Odi could no longer keep his cool. He'd turned into a bundle of nerves, which wasn't like him anymore. So he searched for a rock, and once he found one, he picked it up and took a combative stance. "Who am I? You'd be better off answering that question yourself—Who are you?"

The hyena growled at Odi. "I'll give you the answer to *my* question instead," the hyena hissed. "You are a nobody selected for entertainment as the biggest joke of the year."

The whole pack laughed—typical of hyenas.

Odi got dizzy. That's *impossible. It can't be true …*

Chapter 27

The hyena's crept even closer, and the leader again spoke. "You know it's the truth. There is a regular world; you witnessed it—the world of deserving people living a nice abundant life. And then there are losers like you! The world doesn't need you, and you being such a sap, actually believe in fairy tales. Some hero! Save the world! Help others, blah … blah. Hahaha! Now you're going home, back to the garbage you deserve and have received since the day you were born." The leader growled at Odi, and all the other hyenas slowly crept closer and closer.

Odi's eyes darkened. His heartbeat was pounding in his ears, and he yelled, "You, beast! No one dares to make fun of me! I will strangle you with my bare hands, and you will never get up! I will kill you all right here, right now! Every single one of you!"

Odi shrieked with the injustice of it all, the despair and pain in his soul. The whole world he had acquired today had just collapsed … or, rather, his illusion of it. Odi stood still for a moment, then shouted at the hyena, "Get out of here! What do you want from me?"

The hyenas just laughed and crept closer.

Odi knew he couldn't take them all. "I was pretending, yes, pretending for those chumps to gain trust in me, ok? I just wanted to have some fun, that's all! I'm not stupid, got it? So what's your deal?"

He found himself spewing hateful words, ones he was painfully ashamed of and at the same time feeling hurt from having been deceived by the fairy and the others—he'd been a fool. He noticed that he was coughing up a dark, rotten-smelling substance. He was still filled with bitter anger and was letting it loose. The more Odi yelled, the more of the dark substance he secreted, and a grayish-brown mass fell off his body and hit the ground. One of the smaller hyenas bolted to devour the foul-smelling pile. The beast immediately grew in size. "Good boy," said the leader.

The hyenas gathered around Odi, devouring every angry, evil dark thought and remark, getting larger and fatter with each bite. They no longer bothered talking to him as they greedily gobbled down every dirty bite.

Soon Odi was trapped by the stinky, fat hyenas. The smell of rotten eggs and the tight space made him nauseous. But then, everything seemed to slow down; he could barely hear anything, and his ears were pounding. He suddenly felt like a squeezed-out lemon and was terribly exhausted. At this rate, he'd be dead soon anyway, and leave this world, still unloved and unwanted.

Standing in the middle of the stinking crowd, he lifted his face toward the sky, trying to catch his breath between cursing. That's when he noticed a fragment of bright blue sky. The color reminded him of the shirt he'd worn in the grocery store in his colorful, distant world. As if in a movie, he saw a clear image of his happy face in the future. It was hard to believe it could be his, but it had seemed so natural— It had been him!

"Please help me!" he gasped ... as his rancid world went dark.

Chapter 28

Somehow, it had become more accessible for Odi to breathe. Someone had heard him and came to his rescue. But then, everything spun around in his head, and the events of the entire day ran before his eyes at an accelerated speed.

First, meeting and rescuing a child on the street, then realizing that it was the inner child of the neighbor who had bullied Odi all his life, a magical flashlight, an encounter with his mother's inner child, a golden guardian angel, meeting an honest to goodness fairy on the doorstep of a coffee shop, watching two movies on the wall, meeting the elf, and flying on his magnificent griffin, kids, and their Christmas letters with wishes, Odi as an adult with his family in a grocery store.

Yes, it was all there in his memory. "Everything was real! It all happened!" he shouted. He looked around, noticing that the beasts had calmed down and were slowly fading. They were full and fat, but their eyes were dull again. Some of them belched from gorging themselves. It was over.

The hyenas started to leave. "See you soon!" the pack shouted, laughter echoing from all corners. They quickly moved away from him, dispersed in different directions, then evaporated into thin air.

A few minutes later, Odi returned to his senses and stared ahead blindly. Again, he felt weak and apathetic, desperately wanting to cry but restraining himself.

He sat on the ground and rested his head on his knees, breathing heavily. He wasn't aware of how much time had gone by when someone yelled at him from above.

"Hey, boy, what did you want?"

Odi looked up and saw a curly silver-haired head in one of the windows. "Oh! You must be the lady the fairy spoke of."

"Yeah, that's me. You mentioned something about coffee, didn't you, boy?" asked the lady.

He'd dropped the coffee cup long ago. "Couldn't you hear me before when I called out to you? I thought you didn't exist," In all honesty, he felt relieved that she existed. Perhaps that meant the fairy and the elf hadn't betrayed him, and the hyenas had been lying to him to feed off his anger.

The old woman called, "Yeah, I heard you. I couldn't respond. I was in the middle of something and couldn't leave it. Now I am free."

Odi could feel the spindly fingers of anger creeping towards the edges of his mind.

"So what's with the coffee?" she yelled out of the window. "My friend promised me a coffee. Couldn't you handle that one little thing on your own? What, cat got your tongue?"

That did it. "Listen, granny, I tossed it after waiting for you to answer for over 10-minutes. I kept calling you. You would have gotten it, too, had you not moved as slow as a turtle to respond. So now it's tough patooties for you!" Odi stormed off, making his way back to the coffee shop. He was outraged— with himself mostly. He'd been asked to do a favor by the fairy, and he couldn't even deliver. Crap! But now, he was angry and wanted an explanation for what had just happened with those hyenas.

Odi entered the shop. The fairy and the elf were chatting, giggling, and playing chess. The board was dangling in mid-air, and for some reason, the chess pieces were all wearing different colors, but more importantly, they were tiny human figurines, and they weren't talking but shouting. It seemed the essence of the match was to see who could outshout the other.

The fairy and the elf got quiet as soon as they noticed Odi looking stoned-faced, walking toward them. The figurines also froze, and the chessboard landed with a crash back on the table.

"Odi, what happened? You look awful!" the fairy exclaimed.

"Why did you send me there?" Odi demanded. "So I would fail?"

"Did you fail?" fairy replied more worried now.

The elf kept staring at Odi, dumbfounded. *What was wrong with that boy?*

Odi glared at them. "Oh yes, it took forever when she finally decided to peek out the window when I was near dead from dealing with a pack of hyenas!" He shook his head as if to clear it. "I have no idea how those beasts got into our neighborhood!" Odi blurted out.

"My Fairy," the elf gently interrupted, directing

95

his gaze to Odi's T-shirt. Right above his heart was a dark blob.

The fairy quickly examined the spot and extended her hand to touch it.

Odi stepped back.

Chapter 29

Odi saw their gazes fixed on his chest. "What's wrong?" Odi asked, tilting his chin down, trying to catch a look at his chest.

The fairy walked toward him, looking at Odi with empathy, "Odi, they weren't dogs or any other normal animals."

"What then? You two can't even imagine how tired I am of everything being so mysterious."

"Oh, yes, we can," the fairy replied sternly.

Odi kicked at a small rock. *Where was that when I needed it, he thought sarcastically.* "Really? How so? Were you attacked by a herd of wild dogs, hyenas, or whatever they were? Well, they nearly ate me for dinner while they told me I was a loser and that you all had given me a bullshit story that I believed like a chump!"

Odi felt his blood beginning to boil. "You have no idea how much hate I had for you at that moment! I had no clue how, to tell the truth from lies. How could I trust you? What if you'd decided to trick me? Why would you be so kind to me? Why?"

The fairy waved her hand, and Odi stopped talking—not knowing why.

The elf was hiding behind her, peeking out cautiously.

"Now, you will let me explain," the fairy calmly replied. "I know a lot happened, all at once. But you were strong enough to handle it. Like all other earthly creatures, we each have to go through our own lessons and trials. As for what you call 'hyenas,' they attacked me too long ago, and I won—not right away, but I did. Otherwise, we wouldn't be standing here having this conversation."

Odi felt the fire inside him burn down to a tiny cinder, although he was still tense. "Then tell me who they are," Odi demanded.

The fairy sighed. "They were demons, Odi. They are called different names in different parts of the world, but we'll call them hyena's since those were the avatars they chose to show you. They feed off your dark energy. They don't want people's luminous vitality. That's what kills them. But when you puked up your anger—for the lack of a better word—you threw up anger, hatred, resentment, sarcasm, a desire to kill, slander, revenge, and betrayal. Those are their favorite foods.

When you feel small and insignificant, wishing to destroy yourself and the world, not believing in yourself or others, living in fear, and feeling weak and sorry for yourself, you are serving them their most delicious dessert. They will continue trying to convince you that you don't matter, that you will never succeed, that everyone is the enemy wishing to betray you, and that the world is a scary and evil place just because they want to feed off of you—the more, the better. And their stench is not rotten eggs; it's sulfur."

"What's sulfur?" Odi asked.

The fairy's eyes went dark. "That's what it smells like in hell."

Odi had a lot to think about. A couple of seconds later, he asked, "And now what happens?"

The fairy put the living chess pieces back in their box, "First, your personality and soul get damaged, then your body will follow. They'll stick around and bully you until they suck out all of your energy. They'll convert it into dirty slime and feed on it.

The more you feed them, the more they will come. They want you to be a breeder for them, producing the food necessary for them to thrive. But, of course, they'll still use the others whose negativity they've already gleaned as extra food. Those people have no light or energy left for themselves or for their dreams to come true. The hyenas will do anything to make you waste away, to destroy you and your essence."

"What is my essence?" Odi asked with genuine curiosity.

"Your inner light was gifted to you at birth. The warmth, like the sun, appeared in your heart when you saw the inner child of the cruel or simply cold adults and what you felt for them. You treated them with love and a deep understanding. Your self-esteem and self-worth escalated, and your inner light showed through. Your desire to live and achieve the future of Odi's life livened your step, but you can be sure you won't have it as long as you keep feeding those horrid beasts."

Odi sat down and covered his face with his hands. He felt that all he had done his whole life was experience negative emotions. He never knew anything about his inner light. He had no idea where to look for positivity. "Fairy," he addressed her. "Don't you understand that I will never be able to get rid of them?"

"You are wrong, Odi," the fairy replied.

Odi threw his arms wide. "Oh, really? You and the elf will fly away on the griffin's back far away from here, and I will have to stay. I don't ever want to go back home. What shall I do?" Odi sounded forlorn and alone. There! He saw a shadow out of the corner of his eye. The hyenas had returned.

The fairy noticed them as well. "Odi, you've already started to get rid of them. Otherwise, they wouldn't be so obvious in stalking you. You have gained a great deal of strength, and you can now help others. You saw and saved the inner child of your wrongdoers! Could you have imagined doing something like that even yesterday? The hyenas felt it. They can feel when they are about to lose their food source, so they have returned to scare you and will try to bring you back to feeling the lowest emotions, thoughts, and wishes. They'll do anything to make you lose faith in yourself. Odi, look at me. With my help, we can destroy them!"

That got Odi's attention. "What is it? Are you going to give me some kind of a weapon?" Odi asked, hoping it was something cool like a colorful, futuristic laser weapon or maybe even a stun gun.

"Odi, you already have what you need inside you. Kill them with kindness. All you need to do is stop the negative thoughts that come over you. Tell yourself to stop! Let go of all the negative emotions and thoughts the moment they come over you. That's how you stop feeding them."

The fairy made circular motions on the bar with

her cleaning cloth. "A great way to deal with anger is to identify where it originated in your body. Imagine it as fiery energy. Then you can transform your anger into energy stores for your body. You'll transfer destructive emotions into helpful energy you can use, so the hyenas won't have anything to eat.

And if they have nothing to eat, they will visit you less and less often and eventually stop coming. Now that you've seen them and know who they are, you will find it easier to control them before anger, resentment, fury, or other negative emotions or thoughts can take over. It's called awareness."

"What?" Odi had just about had it with watching his every move all the time. "I'll have to monitor my emotions all the time? Are you serious right now?"

The fairy was exacerbated by Odi's ominous attitude, placing her hands akimbo. "No, you don't have to. You always have a choice. You can stay the same way you are right now and take responsibility for the results. Your second movie, remember? But to be happy and accomplish great things in your life, you must deprive the hyenas of food by controlling your emotions."

Odi went silent.

The fairy continued, "You've been feeding them delicious, lavish meals for a long time. They are used to your food. They will keep coming for the next meal. You have to be strong. Remember what I've told you, be aware, and don't even give them a crumb! It's just a matter of choice—your choice. It will quickly become a good habit. What kind of life will you choose? Which movie? What kind of future? You must remember to try to make wise choices. You are 100 percent responsible for your life!"

Chapter 30

The fairy came to sit on the stool next to him. "Do you remember the world you saw when flying with the griffin on the elf's assignment?"

"Of course!" Odi said, though it seemed so much time had passed since his encounter with the hyenas, it could have been a dream.

"What was your most memorable experience?" the fairy asked.

"I remember the family in the grocery store—me, all grown up with my future family."

"Good. What else?" the fairy asked.

Odi's cheeks flushed with excitement, just thinking about his flight. The speed of the griffin, the weightlessness, the marvelous bright colors, the towns, the people. "The world is so … so vast!" Odi almost whispered. He knew the fairy had seen his thoughts. He could feel her excitement for him. "But my world is tiny, just a gray dot. It is so insignificant. But beyond the gray dot, that's where real life is!"

The fairy clapped her hands together. "Well, then, that's the answer, Odi. There is another world waiting for you; different people, emotions, things to do, and relationships—completely different from your life today. You've seen it. But most importantly, you managed to handle everything that happened alone."

"What do you mean, on my own?" Odi wondered.

"You did it when instead of abandoning the boy, you helped him and another child and yet another. *You* did that, and we—me, the angel, the elf, and the griffin—showed up later."

Odi grew thoughtful. He suddenly felt like the sun had begun to warm him, and soon, pure emotion exploded in his chest more powerfully than ever before. Its sunbeams spread out everywhere, touching everyone's heart.

The Elf couldn't breathe while he witnessed this phenomenon.

Only Odi didn't notice. He looked straight ahead as the corners of his lips were touched by a hardly noticeable smile. A part of him knew that there was no going back now for him. But first, he had to get the hyenas and their stench out of his head. He never wanted to have anything to do with them ever again. He and Dina would drive them away together.

Suddenly he remembered. "Dina!"

"Dina?" the fairy asked.

"Dina, she's my best friend. We were supposed to get together after school, but a lot of time has gone by, and I don't know if she's ok. She'd had a rough night. I'm worried she could be in trouble. But, on the other hand, she's probably been looking for me for a long time. So anyway, I have to go to find her; I'll see you later."

Odi got up and hurried toward the exit. He glanced at his new friends one last time. The angel was with them again, but Odi wasn't surprised. He'd gotten used to his sudden appearances. It seemed like they had known each other their whole lives. *So what will be, will be,* Odi thought.

He glanced at the fairy and could tell by her face that she had read his mind. She nodded, and the elf and the griffin waved goodbye.

Chapter 31

Odi went outside. It was a bright and clear day; he could hear children's faint laughter from nearby. He started walking away from the coffee shop toward home. He planned to charge his phone and try to reach Dina.

The anxiety in his gut grew with each step that took him further away from all the magic he had experienced that day. He was getting closer and closer to his old, gray reality. The magic seemed to be melting away, and the flashlight in the back pocket of his jeans was the only reminder that it hadn't all been a dream. *What will be, will be*, kept singing in his head. He started walking even faster. Finally, he got home.

As soon as he walked inside, he felt the door close on the bright, vast world he had just experienced. The walls of his dwelling seemed even darker and gloomier. Interestingly, Odi thought it was too tight here as if his home had become smaller while he was gone.

Blaring music came blasting from his brother's room. His stepfather was obviously not at home, so naturally, Odi's brother Dan was hanging out with his friends, drinking beer, and playing video games.

His door opened, and cigarette smoke billowed out. Then he saw Odi. "Oh, just in time! Where have you been, scum? Get some sandwiches for us; the money is on the table. Get a move on it, loser, before I get angry."

His brother didn't know that this was the new Odi he was addressing. "No, I'm not going. I have things to do, Dan. Where's Mom?"

His brother was dumbfounded at first. "What? Ah, so you've lost your fear of me, bottom-feeder?" He quickly got angry. "Get on it, dip-wad, before it's too late to escape my anger!" He wiggled his fingers in front of Odi's face. "Dash out now, wiennie, and get our food!"

"Dan, where's Mom?" Odi asked calmly again, trying to keep his brother's anger at bay.

"Who the F *cares where that bitch is?" Dan replied. He belched loudly and lit a cigarette.

"Don't smoke inside the house, please," Odi told himself—*be quiet. You've already said too much.*

"Have you lost your mind, moron?" Dan wasn't expecting Odi's attitude; the cigarette fell out of his mouth, making him even angrier. He came at Odi with his fists clenched. "It looks like you've learned too much at school today, but I haven't taught you a lesson for a while." He punched Odi so hard in the stomach that he curled up in pain.

Odi was raging inside. He remembered running away from the giant, the crying kids, angry parents, and the demonic beasts of the day. He jumped up and yelled at his brother, "Is this your lesson? Really? What do you teach with that?"

Dan's eyes bulged, and his face got red with anger.

His whole body started trembling. "Are you crazy, you dumbass trash?" As he yelled, pieces of the same dirt and slime Odi had already seen with his own eyes— anger, hatred, resentment, fear, revenge, and a desire to kill—started secreting out of Dan's body. Odi saw what was going on, but he couldn't stop it.

And then the same stinky hyenas appeared out of nowhere. They devoured pieces of the dirty energy, fighting for each bite and growling with gluttony. Dan's friends came out of his room to see what was happening.

Chapter 32

"Hey, what the hell is going on out here?" skinny Matt asked.

Dan put his hands on his hips. "Well, my brother here got a little too brave," Dan barked at him. "We need to put him in his place!" he growled as he pulled on his brass knuckles. Fat chunks of slime started pouring from him as the hyenas eagerly rushed to scoop them up.

No one saw them except Odi, who couldn't take his eyes off them—or his brother and his friends. *How can they not see them?* He frantically tried to figure out what to do.

The fairy's voice sounded in Odi's head. "Do not feed them! Make sure there is no food for them!"

He carefully took the angel's feather out of his pocket, and time and space froze. Dan, his friends, and the hyenas froze as well. He needed time to think.

Now he realized how many times the conflicts, fights, and verbal abuse here were provoked and inflated by the hyenas. And the only ones gaining from it were them.

Odi stood there in a daze. Before his eyes, he saw a series of episodes of fights and humiliations that had taken place there over the years, making him and his family suffer, but providing a lot of food for the parasitic hyenas.

Odi noticed a pair of clear, innocent eyes looking at him out of the blue. His brother's inner child was staring at him from the gray box inside him. The child was disheveled, looked exhausted, his face and eyes red—as if he'd been crying for a while; tears were all over his face, and he looked dirty as if his parents had forgotten to bathe him.

The only sound was that of little Dan's sobbing. Odi looked at the young Dan. "Everything is ok now," he said, patting him on his little head. "Listen. Do you realize that you are sitting in a box? Look around you. I know you got used to it and feel safe there, but you need to throw it away. You don't need it anymore. You'll see a different world you can't imagine right now, even in your wildest dreams. But you have the chance to experience it. Once you get rid of that box, I promise you'll discover something wonderful. You'll feel much better. Just believe me, kid, and trust me, please." That Odi was saying this to the inner child of his brother was still pretty confusing, but he knew now that it was true, and the events of today had not been a dream.

Dan's inner child looked at Odi, both suspiciously and hopefully. Then, he climbed out of the box and threw it on the floor. It instantly turned to dust.

"That's better, kid." Odi stroked the little one's hair. "How do you feel now?"

Little Dan smiled at Odi. "I feel very light! I feel like something heavy has dropped off my body. Wow! This feels great! Thank you, bro!" he said, crawling back inside big Dan, then disappeared.

The time started ticking again, and everything came alive.

When Dan and his friends unfroze, they looked at each other, confused, as if they had forgotten why they were there. Odi's older brother looked at his brass knuckles, unsure why he was wearing them. Finally, he took them off and put them in his pocket.

The hyenas came to life snarling and growling. They immediately started in on Odi. "Hey! Where's the food? Why are you waiting? Punch him, punch him," they all shouted in their nasty raspy voices. Finally, one of the hyenas came over to sniff Odi's leg. "What are you waiting for? Show him you're not some sniveling loser!"

"Yes," said another hyena who came to stand beside the other. "Tell him what a big piece of shit he is! Tell him! Tell him! Punch him! Punch him in the face as he's done to you all your life!"

Odi stood still so they wouldn't pounce on him. His eyes watered with tension, but his anger subsided. As the dark energy bits stopped falling from Odi, the hyenas looked at him with anticipation—they'd indeed have a feast if his brother attacked him! If this had happened even yesterday, he'd have definitely done it. But now he realized how they'd all been willing victims of these beasts for years and years.

Odi just looked at them in condemnation. "You're wasting your time here."

The hyena's mouths dropped open in surprise. "Shit!" said one of them.

"What will we do for food," asked another one, and they all stared at their leader. Let's go somewhere else!"

As if in slow-motion, Odi glanced at the hyenas and closed his eyes, trying to follow the fairy's advice and stop them once and for all. All the positive emotions he had experienced, meeting the younger version of his brother, all the good he'd witnessed during the day, the happiness he'd felt, seeing himself all grown up in the grocery store in that different world, ignited the fire in his chest again. The bright, intense sunbeam radiated from his body. Odi understood how it worked now. The rays of the sunbeams reached the hyenas, and one by one, they collapsed and turned into dust. "Good, Odi said."

Odi looked at his brother. "Dan, I am not going to get food for you guys. I have to go to do my stuff," Odi said calmly, cautiously waiting for a reaction.

Odi's brother glanced at him without saying a word, then turned around and went back into his bedroom. His friends followed him.

Chapter 33

With everyone gone, Odi was left alone in the middle of the living room. He exhaled deeply. *Then he thought, Shit, I completely forgot about Dina! I have to go!*

He kept calling Dina on the way to her house, but there was no answer. The closer he got, the more anxious he felt.

Dina lived in a small one-floor house surrounded by more little houses not far from their school. When Odi arrived, the place was dark. He knocked on the door. Strangely enough, Dina opened it right away. The girl looked a mess, her face and eyes puffy and red. She'd been crying for a while. Her lip was severely bruised.

"Dina, what happened?" Odi asked, putting his hand on her shoulder.

She shrugged it off. "What do you care?" Dina angrily replied, stepping outside and closing the door behind her.

"Because I am your friend, and I care. Tell me," Odi insisted. It was the same Dina he saw at school this morning, but he knew something had happened again.

Something had taken place within him as well. He viewed everything differently now—colors, sounds, smells, but most importantly, he saw her differently. She looked so lost and beaten down, and he sympathized with her to the depths of his core. It was the first time he'd ever felt this way. Yesterday, he would have only felt anger and the need to fight for her.

Suddenly, he spotted Dina's inner child. She was in a gray box, in the fetal position. He could see the terror in her tear-stained eyes and depleted gaze. The little girl was staring at him. Odi wasn't surprised. He looked at Dina, waiting for her to answer.

Dina crossed her arms over her chest. "You're supposed to be my friend, dude. Why didn't you come to meet me, as we'd agreed?" she said through clenched teeth. She seemed afraid to raise her voice, maybe not wanting to wake someone …

"What do you mean?" Odi asked. "I was there, and you weren't!"

"No," Dina interrupted, "I went, but you weren't there. I left. On my way home, I realized I didn't have my cell phone; I guess the bastards at school stole it. So I wasn't able to call you." She wiped her nose. She was holding back tears and hadn't told him what had happened to her.

Odi was concerned about how she looked. "And then? What happened after? Why do you look like this?" asked Odi.

Dina swung around with clenched fists. "Ok, already! My father wasn't here when I got home, but my mother was—drunk. She beat me up and called me a slut. That's it. Simple. What did you expect?"

She suddenly burst out laughing. "I told you, Odi, that's what I am now! My father has turned me into a slut. He told my mother that when they were fighting, and he said I lured him! So they are going to have some fun with my life now. My mother told me she would start pimping me out. That way, she'll get some use out of me."

The girl continued to laugh hysterically, louder and louder.

Odi looked around, frightened.

Dina was still shaking with laughter, but it quickly turned into hysterical sobbing. She soon plopped down on the porch steps, put her head on her knees, and covered her face with her hands.

Chapter 34

Odi sat beside her, trying to soothe her, but she pushed him away.

"Don't you dare touch me! I am a dirty slut, don't you get it?"

"Dina, I need to tell you something!" Odi exclaimed.

"Get out of here!" Dina replied.

"Dina," Odi started. He was dying to tell her about everything he'd experienced today, but he was cautious. *This is probably not the right time to tell her that story now. What if she thinks I've taken some drugs?* He couldn't just let it all out without thinking it over first.

There was an uncomfortable silence between them. "What should I do now?" Dina asked, feeling doomed. Her eyes filled with an unhealthy fire.

"I ..." Odi began.

Dina turned to him and asked bluntly, "Will you help me kill them? Yes! That's it. You can help me; it will be easier to get it done if we do it together. Then I'll be clean again and get rid of my shameful past! Yeah, we'll plan it carefully, and no one will ever find out. It will be our little secret and … ."

"Dina, no!" Odi interrupted, but it was too late. He saw the dark slime falling off of her. "Crap, anything but that!" Odi hissed.

She sniffed and started crying again. "Why not? Don't you want me to get my innocence back and be free of them?"

"You are innocent now, Dina!" Odi exclaimed. He wanted to cry right along with her, but he restrained himself. This was not the time to cave. "Nothing is your fault, Dina. How can you think that? And it's not their fault either!" he blurted out.

Dina jumped to her feet. "What? What's not *their* fault? How can you say that? I hate them." She stamped her feet. "Hate them! Hate them!" Dina was screeching, getting herself into a rage.

Odi saw the slime pour out of her. "Shh! Dina, please stop," Odi whispered, sounding alarmed. He looked at her, thinking something horrible was about to happen—and he was right.

As soon as the thought crossed his mind, giant hyenas like the ones he'd been feeding his energy to his entire life appeared.

Dina couldn't see them, even though they were right before her. At first, two, then three, and more beasts appeared. Soon Odi counted a dozen.

"Yummy, yummy, food!" cackled the hyenas as they greedily devoured the slime.

Odi jumped up. "No, Dina, please stop, calm down!" he yelled, staring at the hyenas.

Dina paused, watching Odi concentrate and intensely stare at an empty spot. "Stop what?" she yelled even louder. "Hey Odi, look at me. I just said I need your help! We can do it now! My mother is asleep—

we can take care of her right now!"

Another big fat piece of slime fell out of her. The hyenas jumped to grab it, knocking each other over and growling over the nasty, stinking morsel.

Without Dina's cooperation, he knew all he'd be able to do was watch the horror unfold.

"Dina, *stop feeding them!* Stop it, or it will never end!"

"What? Who should I not feed, Odi? What the hell? Have you been eating mushrooms? What's going on with you? Hello?" Dina yanked Odi by his sleeve.

Chapter 35

Odi grabbed the flashlight from his pocket and shone it at the hyenas.

Dina jumped up as if she'd been struck by lightning. "What are they? Dogs? Are they—Where did they come from? The stench, how disgusting!" She pinched her nostrils shut. "PU! What's going on here?"

Suddenly one of the beasts glared at Odi and yelled, "What are you standing here for? Where is the food? Give us more food! Give us more food!"

Lowering its voice to a hissing sound, another beast added with a grin, "What are you staring at? Did you fall for the fairy tale? The witch mixed some drug into your coffee to fill your head with nonsense, and you, being stupid, fell for it! Someone like you has no future. You are a piñata for beatings until you learn to fight so well that they'll leave you alone! Jail would be the best-case scenario for you! They feed you on the house, and you don't have to do anything!"

"Yes, yes, jail is a way to go for you and this little, dirty whore!" the third hyena said, and they all burst into disgusting laughter.

Odi felt his stomach clench and rage spilling into his veins. "You beasts!" He instinctively clenched his fists and spit out the answer, "Come here. I am going to tear your stinking mouths off!" He took a step forward, and a big ball of black slime rolled off him.

The fastest hyena grabbed it and gobbled it in one big bite. "Here we go. Yum, yum, yum. Good boy," croaked the hyena.

Odi quickly stopped and stood still. The coldness radiating from him spread out all over his body. Then, suddenly, as if he'd just come out of a trance, his mind cleared. "Stop! I got it! They are provoking me!"

Dina stared at him, speechless. She looked back at the hyenas and again at him.

"I got this, Dina! They provoke us, so they have something to eat! Now I will handle them."

Dina still stood there in shock, her mouth hanging open.

Odi took a deep breath and, closing his eyes, said, "Love and empathy. All at once."

The bright sun inside him lit up, quickly spreading through his chest.

What happened next changed Dina's life forever.

Huge sunbeams protruded from within Odi's chest and spread out in every direction, reaching the hyenas. As soon as the rays touched them, the beasts blew up, turned to dust, and evaporated. There were no sounds now, but the nasty smell of sulfur lingered in the air for a while as a reminder of what had just taken place. It was over.

Odi smiled. "Wow, that's really how to kill with kindness!" He tried to catch his breath. His heart was pounding. He'd done it. They'd done it. Dina was a big part of this victory since she'd followed Odi's request to stop and believe. They had won.

Dina swallowed and stared at him, her eyes wide with fear.

It was quiet for a moment. Then, suddenly, a loud clapping of hands came from behind them, breaking the silence.

Odi quickly turned around—it was his angel, and apparently, he'd brought another angel. It was a girl, and she looked a lot like—Dina!

The angels were dressed identically—their clothes made from the same light, golden cloth. The girl angel even had the same wings on her back as Odi's angel.

"I told you he'd be able to stop her!" Odi's angel said, addressing the girl angel.

"Yay! Finally!" the girl angel cheered with a luminous smile.

Dina looked at the couple. She rolled her eyes at Odi. There were big questions in her eyes. "Friends of yours?"

Odi laughed at the look on her face. "Oh, Dina, I have so much to tell you! But first, meet my guardian angel, and what seems to be your guardian angel as well," said Odi with a deep breath, knowing he had a lot of explaining to do.

The angels smiled and waved at them, then vanished.

Chapter 36

Dina was stunned by all she'd just seen. She turned to Odi. "People come and go so quickly here, don't they?"

"I can explain."

She folded her arms across her chest. "Oh, yes, please do. I'm waiting with bated breath."

Odi told her everything he had experienced that day. How he met and rescued a little boy who turned out to be his neighbor's inner child; how he got the flashlight, which had helped Dina see the hyenas and had helped him to see the inner child inside everyone—including his abusers.

He described the gray boxes of repressed feelings and talked about the angel, the fairy, the elf, the massive griffin, and his magical ride on him. He explained the kids' letters to Santa, Christmas wishes, and how he'd seen himself with the beautiful family at the grocery store. About the gray world and how beyond the gray world was another, a limitless universe that Dina needed to experience too. She needed to discover the truth.

Dina listened intently without saying a word, nodding at times. Odi thought she understood him until she said, "So, let me get this straight, you helped your neighbor who has beaten you up for years? That piece of shit we were planning to teach a lesson to one day so that he wouldn't be able to hurt anyone ever again? Really?"

Odi was taken aback by her tone. "Dina, I helped the little boy inside him, his inner child, who'd been through a lot in the past." Odi pursed his lips. How could he expect Dina to understand everything when he'd found it hard to believe that he'd saved someone who had nearly killed him before? "I ... "

Dina's unexpected outburst interrupted Odi's thoughts. "Wow, you're high, right? What did you take? I want some too! I want to have a fairy tale like this!" She laughed hysterically. "Those guys gave you some shit, right?" Dina said, pointing to where the angels stood only minutes ago. "Oh ... are your angels gone?" she said, laughing sarcastically. "Come on, Odi! Either share that shit with me or get the hell out of here!

She stood. "You are useless today. I need to figure out how to—" She stopped and looked around. "How are we going to get out of here and take care of everything if you're too busy babysitting some kids and high as F!" She started to leave him.

"Dina, wait!" Odi pulled the flashlight out of his pocket and handed it to her.

"Take it, and shine it at me."

Dina rolled her eyes but took the flashlight and shone it at him. Her eyes grew wide in terror, but she found she couldn't close them. "Oh shit! What's in there?" Dina whispered, frightened.

"That's my inner child. He is always in there," Odi calmly replied. "He is already out of the box and feeling better. Now, it's your turn." He took the flashlight and shone it at Dina.

She was terrified, looking through her chest down to her belly. But, first, she saw a box.

Odi pushed the flashlight closer, and the beam illuminated the box. Dina could see a baby girl inside, staring at her with fearful, puffy eyes.

"Whoa, Whoa, Whoa!" Dina shouted. "How is this possible? Dina was about to cry, but Odi's soft voice stopped her.

"Hi, baby girl," Odi said gently to the baby in the box. "Everything will be fine now. I'm here to help you. But to do that, we need to get you out of that yucky box. It is a terrible place, trust me. Come on, just climb out of there."

The little girl held onto the box even tighter and covered her face.

"The trauma is too severe. It's going to take time," Odi said, surprised by his own words. He pulled himself together and continued looking at Dina. "Go inside, Dina, and look at your mother; use the flashlight. You'll discover something about her and meet someone really special."

Dina glanced at Odi. "What is going on here? What is this?"

Odi pulled her to her feet. "Dina, please, you need to see what I'm talking about. Just trust me. I am your friend. Just trust me and do it. We will talk about everything else later. Come on, do it, please?" Odi handed her the flashlight.

Dina took a deep breath, silently grabbed the flashlight from his hand, and went inside the house.

Odi followed her.

She walked down the hall and straight into her mother's bedroom. It was dark and smelled like alcohol and cigarettes. The only light in there came from a tiny nightlight in the bathroom.

Dina's mother was sleeping on her side, a full ashtray lying on the bed beside her. Dina always worried she'd fall asleep with a lit cigarette and cause a fire.

Dina approached the bed, turned on the flashlight, and directed the light at her mother.

Chapter 37

The first thing she saw was a gray box inside her mother. Dina opened her eyes wide. She got closer, still pointing to the light. Now she could see through the box. There was a little girl inside, hiding in the very bottom corner. She shaded her eyes with her little hands from the bright light, looking at Dina in fear.

The little girl looked exhausted, and her eyes were red and swollen from crying. She looked so pathetic and downtrodden that Dina's first thought was to help her. But instead, she swallowed the lump in her throat as her tears threatened to choke her.

Dina looked over her mother's body and felt hostility and hatred overcome her again. But then the flashlight shone on the gray box again, and she just couldn't ignore the little girl inside, so she got closer and stared at her.

Odi watched silently from outside the door.

Dina stood quietly, looking down at the baby girl. Tears flowed from her eyes. "Hello, little one. You've been here all this time waiting for someone to find you … oh no … don't be afraid of me, I won't hurt you," Dina whispered.

Her mother's inner child quietly sobbed. Dina got closer. The child moved even further into the corner. Suddenly the flashlight itself pulled Dina's hand up and shone a beam on the wall. Then a movie started, and Dina watched in amazement as it unfolded.

It looked like an old movie in black and white. The movie was about Dina's mother, Cara. A baby girl had been born and refused by her mother. She was only eighteen. Her father and his mother took care of the poor baby. Grandma replaced the mother and cared for the little one full-time because her father was only nineteen. It showed scenes from her childhood. But, of course, she lacked the attention from her father because he was simply too young to care for her.

Now it was Christmas Eve in the living room of this house. Dina knew that the house she lived in used to belong to her grandma. She saw everything the little girl had experienced since birth, first as a toddler and now as old as Dina. She was in the living room, watching old movies, and her father was beside her on the sofa.

He was melting something in a spoon with the lighter. Filling a syringe with the liquid from the spoon, he squeezed his hand with an elastic band and plunged the syringe into a swollen vein, squeezing out the contents. He leaned back in euphoria and closed his eyes.

Young Cara had no idea what was happening beside her; she was watching an old Christmas movie and laughing from time to time. Then, after a few moments, her father's head fell to the side and struck her on the shoulder. His hand opened, and the syringe fell into the ashtray with a clatter.

The girl turned to him. There, she saw her father's motionless, limp body slumped on the sofa next to her. His face was pasty white from the drug overdose, and the skin around his nose and upper lip had turned a dark blue. He was gone.

"Dad? Dad?" she shook him, but he didn't move. "Dad?" She gazed at the syringe in the ashtray and picked it up.

"What is this? Dad?" She touched his shoulder, but he didn't respond.

Hysteria began to bubble up inside her. "Dad, are you okay? What is going on? Dad, wake up, wake up, you're scaring me. Please wake up!" Cara's voice was raspy from shouting, and hot tears gushed from her eyes while she shook his shoulders. His eyes were closed, and white foam began to flow from his open mouth.

There was no one home except for them.

Cara rushed about the room in a panic, realizing that something terrible had happened to her father, but she didn't know how to help him. Then she ran back to him and pulled his eyelid up. There, staring back at her, was a dull, lifeless eye in which there was almost no pupil. Cara's father had been only thirty-two.

He was as cold as ice. Cara fell to her knees next to her father's dead body, screaming into her hands. "No!" There was so much pain and despair in her scream that Dina sobbed in turn. She knew that her grandfather had died young of a heroin overdose, but she had no idea it had happened at Christmastime. That explained why her mom hated Christmas so much and was always drunk and high on that holiday

The movie flashed very quickly after that. Her mother sat next to her dead father until her grandma came home. Her relationship with her grandmother was forever spoiled after that.

Feelings of guilt for her father's death, coupled with the feelings of worthlessness and uselessness instilled by a grieving grandmother whose mentality had been destroyed by the death of her only son.

Due to neglect and despair, Cara had begun strolling through the streets with bad company, alcohol, and drugs to ease those feelings. The flashlight turned off.

Dina stood in a daze with tearful eyes. She felt the sharp pain of empathy bubble in her throat as it threatened to burst forth.

Odi, standing outside the door all this time, came in and gave her a big hug. The unspoken words between them made him sigh heavily into her hair. "All cruel adults had a very difficult childhood ... all of them. Now you will understand this."

Dina sobbed on his shoulder.

"Now, let's help your mom's inner child," Odi said, taking her hand. They both knew now that Dina's mom had suffered much bitterness and resentment for many years.

Odi took the flashlight from Dina's hand and pointed it at Dina's mother, still lying on the bed.

The light again illuminated the box and the little girl inside. The little girl was used to the nasty box. It was an excellent place for her to hide from the hyenas, which were always around.

Dina tried to catch her breath not to frighten her mother's inner child. "Don't be afraid, little one, please. We are here to help you. You need to get out of the box," she said, slowly getting closer.

The little girl wasn't convinced, and her bottom lip started trembling.

"It's not working," Dina whispered desperately.

Quite unexpectedly, Dina's inner child stepped out from inside her like a glowing hologram. She looked at her older self and then walked toward her mother, extending her hands. "Hello, Cara ... I am Dina, and I want to help you." She smiled at the little girl inside the box.

The look in the little one's eyes was so innocent that a strange feeling came over big Dina, and she felt her heart grow. Hot tears rolled down her cheeks.

Odi came up behind them. "Baby girl, you need to trust little Dina and come out of that nasty box," he coaxed.

Little Dina stretched out her hands to the girl. "Hey, come on, I am here to help. Let me help you come out of there."

Her mother's inner child timidly held her hand out to little Dina—timidly at first. Then, to their surprise, she climbed out of the box, dropping it on the floor. The box evaporated into thin air. Both girls rejoiced and sat on the floor facing each other.

Little Dina hugged little Cara tightly to her. She could feel her little body trembling. "Here you go, baby ... here you go ... now isn't that much better?" asked little Dina, as she swayed side to side, embracing Cara. Little Dina and Cara hugged for a few more minutes. Then the little girls happily smiled at each other.

Big Dina was crying on Odi's shoulder again.

Dina and Odi couldn't take their eyes off the little ones. Everyone was smiling, warmed by empathy, compassion, and love.

Odi's guardian angel clapped his hands, breaking in on their resolve. Everyone turned and stared at Dina's and Odi's guardian angels, who had appeared and were accompanied by little Cara's guardian angel.

"Bravo! Bravo to all!" he thundered so loud that the other two angels held their hands over their ears.

Odi looked at Dina. "They'll always be next to us, watching after us."

Dina looked up at Odi. "What does all this mean?" she asked. Her tone had become very pensive.

Odi smiled. "That's what I was trying to tell you. I went through the same thing earlier today, and at first, I didn't understand any of it ... But then I got it.

Dina, you need to know that nothing in your life has been your fault. It happened because the children who were abused or hurt in the past grew up and started hurting the weaker ones. And the ones who hurt them had also suffered before. Inside, every evil, aggressive, cold person is a formerly abused, wounded, and upset child. When these children become adults, they don't know any other way besides how they were treated, just like the little girl that lived inside your mother."

Odi put the flashlight back in his pocket, and Dina, her mother's inner child, and the angels disappeared.

"Now what? How do I handle it from here?" Dina asked Odi with hope.

"It's all about choices," he replied. "All you can do is make good choices. And your choices will impact your life forever. When you choose not to continue along your old path, when you can see a crying child inside each rude and angry adult, your life will drastically change. Then, finally, you'll have a chance to live in abundance and happiness and leave this hole for good," Odi said in an adult manner.

Dina looked at her friend, absorbing every word.

Chapter 38

They quietly left her mother's room and retreated to the living room. Odi plunked down on the sofa.

Dina let out a yelp when she noticed a tiny man with a funny facial expression and a thermos in his hand, standing right next to Odi.

Odi heard Dina's sudden outburst and followed the direction of where she was staring. But instead, he found himself staring into those of the elf standing on the armrest next to him.

The elf held out a paper cup to Dina. "I brought you some hot tea, young lady," he said. He tried to bow gracefully, but it looked funny.

Dina brushed up against Odi. "Who's the guy in the funny little hat?" she asked. "You do see him, right?" she wondered. "Do you know him?"

Odi smiled. "Yes, of course! Dina, meet my friend the elf. Elf, meet my friend Dina."

The elf nodded his head at Dina knowingly. "Oh, this must be the young lady you're keeping in your mind! I am the elf. Oh, here … have some tea—it has special healing powers!" he exclaimed.

Dina brought the paper cup to her lips, staring at Odi, who nodded. She took a sip. It was delicious. It tasted like cherries, vanilla, and something undetectable—something tart but with a fantastic taste. She took another sip and exhaled. A warm feeling came over her as the warmth of the tea spread throughout her body. "What were you saying about changing one's life, my dear friend?" she asked Odi.

Dear friend? The calming effect of the tea on Dina made him have to clear his throat to stifle a chuckle. "Ahem, I was saying that you are now at the crossroads of your life where you must make an important decision. Do you want to continue on the road of anger, and keep your inner child in a box made with hate, go on feeding the nasty, gluttonous hyenas, and let your life roll downhill? You witnessed what that could be like. Or you can direct your new life towards the other road, where it will be filled with light, happiness, and abundance to help you fulfill your mission in this world."

Dina listened to Odi very carefully. He seemed utterly different now. His speech, facial expressions, and eyes were different. So bright and clear.

Odi continued, "We also have a lot of helpers and guardians around us. Your guardian angel is always by your side, always trying to help," Odi said knowingly and, turning around, looked for his. He immediately appeared.

Dina also turned around and stared at her angel.

Both angels shook their heads approvingly. "I am always around," Dina's angel said, giving her a warm smile.

Dina's expression turned cold. "Always around?

Really? Where were you every time my father was raping me? Why did you allow it? Why didn't you help me?! Why?! Dina's voice faltered as she felt a sharp pain in her throat from choking back the hot tears that threatened to come. She covered her face with her hands. "Why me? Why me?"

Odi looked questioningly at her angel and then locked eyes with his own in question.

The angel stroked Dina's hair lovingly. "Dina, I understand your pain, and of course, I know everything you've been through," her angel replied. "It is not within my power to change or control the events that happen to you. Only you can change your life. I can only support you in any way I can, with any of your decisions."

Dina opened her palms and looked up at her angel with tear-stained eyes. "Tell me! Why is this happening to me? Why?" she demanded.

Her angel came to stand next to her. "Well, my dear, to understand, let's look at your father. Odi, please give Dina the flashlight."

He pulled the flashlight out of his pocket and handed it to her.

"Dina, point the light at the wall, please," her angel said.

Dina sniffed, wiped away her tears, then obediently took the flashlight, aiming its beam at the wall.

Instantly, images appeared on the wall.

A small boy was alone in his room with his building blocks. A man entered the room with a flask in his hands. It was clear that he was drunk. The boy was happy to see his dad. Then the man babbled something as he came closer to the boy. Suddenly he stopped in front of the boy and pulled his pants down … the flashlight turned itself off.

"What!!!" Dina started shaking all over and thought she might faint.

Odi rushed to her side. "Enough! Can't you see she's just been traumatized?"

"She needs to see to understand," her angel said. "That was your father, Dina. His father (your grandpa) raped him all through his childhood. His psyche was shattered long ago, so he transferred what was done to him to you. He is repeating his traumatized psyche. So it has nothing to do with you. It is not your fault."

The angel came to Dina. "This is how it is. In most cases, every abused child becomes an adult with a traumatized psyche. That is how it comes down the chain. Now that you realize this, you have the opportunity to break out of this vicious cycle of repetition. Please don't become a victim or an aggressor because that would be very sad. Despite this terrible experience, you can remain a peaceful and compassionate person who understands why this has happened and show your true power this way."

Dina listened attentively, calming her little by little.

Odi took her hand. "Dina, it was hard for me, in the beginning, to see other venues and think other ways," Odi admitted. "It felt like something was breaking inside me … it was bizarre to feel compassion for my offender. But once you learn to see them inside as the offended, wounded, love-deprived inner child, you will never be the same."

He stood at the window and looked out. "I also broke down, but when I finally experienced compassion, it was incredibly powerful," said Odi. "The moment you experience it, you'll find yourself entering a different dimension."

Odi turned from the window to face her. "There is a lot of light here and all sorts of helpers. The elf, for example." Odi pointed to the elf, who was still sipping his tea. "The elf is one of Santa's helpers."

"What?" Dina opened her mouth in amazement. "I thought you were just one of Odi's friends. So you're one of Santa's helpers? That is truly amazing!"

The elf's face turned beet red with embarrassment. "Yes, I'm the top elf, well, almost the top, and since Odi helped me, I will be awarded that position for sure! But I am going to repay Odi for his help!" the elf eagerly announced, giving Odi a tiny high-five.

Odi turned back to Dina. "So, my friend, the sooner you choose the path of light, the more wonderful opportunities will come your way. And those dirty, rotten hyenas will stop coming. Quite the contrary, you will meet many wonderful people and magic will enter your life. The elf and your guardian angel are part of that magic."

Dina smiled slightly.

"Let's go outside," said the elf.

They followed him through the door.

The Elf looked shy and said: "Let's go see the fairy! It's time you two met. Now, where is that lazy bones flying around … where is my griffin?" The elf looked up at the sky, preoccupied.

The teens followed his gaze into the heavens.

Chapter 39

Dina stood mesmerized as a giant beast flew into view above them. It was love at first sight. She thought she'd never seen anything as beautiful as the griffin, wiggling his vast wings on his way down.

"Finally!" The elf threw his hands in the air in frustration.

The griffin landed right next to them. Dust flew, and Odi and Dina coughed and sneezed.

"Who ... is this magnificent creature?" Dina asked nervously, her voice trembling.

"This is a griffin. He's my friend," said Odi, patting the strange animal on his feathered neck.

"Let's get ready to fly on him to visit the fairy!" the elf announced and gestured for everyone to climb aboard the beautiful creature.

The griffin stared curiously at Dina with his huge emerald eyes.

Dina stood dazed, looking at the strange animal. "He has the head and wings of an eagle, but the body of a lion?" she asked in disbelief.

The griffin lowered his massive head to allow them access to climb aboard.

Odi patted the griffin's massive head feathers. "Yes, this is a griffin, a mythical, magical animal. He is very kind and very bright. He understands everything said to him and flies fast. But he has a fish obsession, don't you boy," Odi said, patting the griffin's neck. He laughed. "Come on, let's go! He motioned to Dina and the elf. "I can't wait for you to meet the fairy," he said, climbing on the griffin.

"Yes!" the elf eagerly replied. "She's been waiting all day to meet you."

"I can't wait to meet her!" Dina said anxiously.

He hoisted Dina up beside him on the massive animal. "Don't be afraid; he's as gentle as a kitten!"

"I am going my own way up on him, don't worry about me!" the elf yelled as they were about to take off.

"Dina, hold on tight to me!" shouted Odi.

The griffin pushed off with sturdy paws and spread his enormous wings as they soared into the air.

Dina almost fell off but managed to cling to Odi.

Odi patted the griffin on his massive neck. "Whoa, hold on, buddy. Let's take it easy. We have a lady on board!" yelled Odi to the griffin.

The colossal animal softened his manner of flying as they flew higher above the puffy white clouds.

The coffee shop was not far from Dina's house by air, but it would have been a long walk.

Dina was captivated by the flight. Airstreams whistled past her in the face. She felt like they were blowing away her previous life. It was unforgettable!

Dina's mind was spinning. She felt like her brain was creaking from processing all of these actions. But, finally, she just let it go and surrendered herself to the airflow and the smooth swaying of the griffin.

They landed next to the coffee shop a couple of minutes later.

Chapter 40

The Fairy greeted them at the door. It was getting dark, and the coffee shop looked different with the vintage lanterns on.

"Hello. Hello. Welcome!" the fairy said, smiling. Odi jumped off of the griffin and helped Dina to the ground.

Dina seemed to be in a trance from everything that was happening.

"Dina, this is the fairy ... a real one!" said Odi, peering carefully into her eyes in anticipation of her reaction.

"It's wonderful to finally meet you, Dina," replied the fairy. "Odi speaks very highly of you."

Dina slowly walked toward her and cautiously stared back and forth between Odi and the fairy. She curtsied and said, "It is very nice to meet you, Madam," Dina said shyly.

The fairy smiled. "It seems you've had a very long day, my dear. Come in, and I will feed you. I also have an amazing selection of hot drinks. Did you like my tea, Dina?" she said, leading them inside the coffee shop.

"Yes, the one the elf gave me was amazing," said Dina, getting frustrated at saying, "the elf."

The fairy noticed her frustration. "Let's go, my dears!" she said cheerfully and walked inside the coffee shop, gesturing for the others to follow.

The mood inside felt subdued, with the cozy lighting and real candles burning all around. Against the far wall sat a large brick fireplace with a natural fire burning in it. It looked more like an old castle than a modern coffee shop. It smelled of vanilla, pastry ... and all things sugar and spice.

Odi remembered this morning when he'd come here the first time as if it had happened in a past life. But, of course, everything was in the past, just not so long ago. The fear that the gray life would soon return hadn't subsided yet.

Odi came to stand beside Dina. "Don't be afraid. Everything is going to be fine; I promise you," he said, reading Dina, who seemed agitated, stomping in place, and unsure whether to come in.

When they finally entered, Dina, just like Odi at first, stood closest to the exit.

The fairy pretended not to notice. "I have an amazing hot apple pie with ice cream for you guys. Would you like another herbal tea or coffee, my dear?" she asked Dina.

"Me? ... Yes, I think I would like another tea, thank you," Dina replied

"Right away," the fairy addressed the girl and nodded to the elf. He hurried behind the bar.

"Would you like to sit here?" the fairy said, pointing to a beautifully set table. Odi and Dina obediently sat down.

The elf appeared from behind the bar with two

cups on little saucers. With the steam came incredible smells of fresh herbal tea and rich, strong coffee intertwined in a fantastic combination.

The elf carefully placed the steaming cups in front of Odi and Dina.

"Here is your tea and coffee," said the elf, setting the cups in front of them.

The fairy offered them crispy warm apple pie on small, beautiful China plates. Fragrant smells of cinnamon and freshly baked apples rose to tease the pallet and were nestled in among generous scoops of vanilla ice cream.

"Eat quickly, my dears, before the ice cream melts," said the fairy on her way back to the counter, giving Dina enough time to get comfortable.

Dina was hungry and greedily swallowed her piece, whispering to Odi, "Is all of this for us?"

Odi nodded appreciatively.

The fairy watched them from the counter while drinking a fresh coffee.

Having eaten three slices of tasty pie, Dina got more comfortable.

The fairy noticed and slowly approached them, "Did you enjoy the pie, my dear?" the fairy asked Dina.

"Oh, yes. This is the most delicious apple pie I've ever tasted in my life," she replied.

"I'm glad you liked it, my dear. I baked it myself, especially for you two," the fairy said as she sat at their table.

"Really? For us? You knew we were coming?" asked Dina, surprised, moving her gaze to Odi as she looked for assurance that she was safe.

"Yes, I did," said the fairy, who paused and looked into Dina's soulful eyes.

Dina again looked at Odi questioningly.

"She knows everything, Dina. So you can trust her," said Odi.

"Yes, I am here to help you, my dear. You saw the flashlight, which shed a lot of light on some new things today, and you are upset." She continued. "I'm sure it was way too much all at once, and you are confused."

"Yes, this is all very strange," Dina agreed.

The fairy patted Dina's hand. "It's never easy to look at everything objectively while looking into the root cause of something. So I know you have very mixed feelings inside right now," said the fairy with understanding.

"Yes," responded Dina. "That's exactly how I feel. Odi and that angel told me a lot of things and showed me a lot with the flashlight," said Dina. "I realized that my mother and father had challenging experiences in their childhood. I saw it. It was shocking. Horrible. I felt bad for them. But ... "

The fairy nodded in understanding. "But you are very hurt by what they've done to you," said the fairy.

Dena suddenly slapped her hand down on the table. "Yes, I am! I'm hurt! I am very damn hurt!" Tears welled up in Dina's eyes. "I hate that asshole for what he did to me! Yes, I do! And I have the right to feel that way!" She threw her napkin on the table. "Why should I care and understand that he has a suffering child inside who was raped his whole childhood? Why does he do it to me, then? He knows how it feels!"

Dina felt the lump in her throat, and tears welled up in her eyes. "He's just a cruel prevent who is sick in his head! Why should I be understanding but not him?" Dina began to shake, gripped by suffering and pain.

"Dina, no!" Odi said, trying to stop her.

"Yes! The truth is that I want to tie him up and cut him into pieces! And I would do it slowly and start it with his filthy cock! Yes! And do you know what? Watching him suffer from pain would be a real pleasure!" Dina clenched her fists and pursed her lips from the anger that captured her.

Odi shook his head at her disapprovingly.

She poked her finger at Odi's chest. "You were going to help me with that, bro! What happened to you?" she asked Odi.

Odi let out a sigh. "Not anymore," he replied.

"Oh yes!"

Suddenly, everyone heard scratching on the glass and turned around.

The large windows filled quickly with hyenas who stood on their hind legs behind the glass, crawling on top of one another to see. They showed their sharp fangs and leered at them. They seemed particularly interested in Dina, their red, hungry eyes glowing in the darkness.

Thick, brown slime dripped from their mouths and oozed down the glass. Finally, some light from the side illuminated them, and in addition to their terrible red, glowing eyes and silhouettes, their filthy fangs were visible.

"There you go, Dina. Your friends are waiting for you just outside!" said the fairy. "They will not dare enter here, but as soon as you leave, they will start hanging around with you all the time."

Dina opened her eyes wide and covered her mouth with her palm, realizing what she'd just done.

"Do you want to go to them? They will listen to your speech with pleasure … pleasure for them because it will mean plenty of food for them," said the fairy.

"I don't want to go outside," whispered Dina in desperation.

The fairy circled her. "Interesting. You know that they exist, yet you must still want to feed them … so, do you want them to be around you?" the fairy asked.

Dina was ashamed of her conduct. "No, I don't … I just—forgot. I'm just telling you how I feel!" said Dina, confused.

"I understand that it is challenging for you and much easier to slip into these feelings of negativity and anger. That you quite simply got used to it. But now you know that the hyenas incite and provoke it. Most people don't even realize this; they don't see the hyenas and don't realize they exist. But you do, Dina. You know all about them, and you can see them right now," said the fairy.

"Yes … I do … but," Dina mumbled.

"Try to understand, child," interrupted the fairy. "Those hyenas are just a part of what is coming to you if you continue to 'forget.'

Let me show you something. Odi, please hand me the flashlight."

Chapter 41

Odi pulled the flashlight from his back pocket.

The fairy looked toward the windows with the snapping hyenas and fluttered her hand as if pushing something out into the air. The hyenas hurried away from her movement as if running from a crashing wave.

Odi handed her the flashlight and glanced at Dina. He could only imagine the emotions she was about to experience.

"Give it to Dina," the fairy said. "Let's get closer to the wall." The fairy pointed at the same place Odi had viewed his two movies. "Switch it on, dear."

Dina sat down, switched on the flashlight, and shone it at the wall.

A marvelous story developed. A wonderful young woman was designing clothes. She worked a lot, formed successful partnerships with others, and eventually entered the high fashion scene. Soon she became well-known all over the world. She traveled a lot, became wealthy, and had a beautiful home. She met a fantastic man and created a beautiful, happy family with him.

Dina watched, mesmerized. Her heart was beating fast. Every scene made her feel warm inside as she absorbed everything she saw.

Odi was watching Dina. It seemed that she was basking in the bright light of fulfillment. But he knew the second movie would start soon.

The first scene of the second movie was completely different and in another genre altogether. Within the gray walls of a shabby apartment, a beat-up woman sat on a dirty bed, pouring booze into a filthy glass. A little girl was crying in the corner.

Dina's heart sank. She pushed away from the table and curled herself into a ball on the back of the chair. She didn't want to continue watching, but at the same time, it was too compelling for her to want to turn away. It was as if whatever was going to happen in the movie depended on her.

The fairy nodded. "That's right, Dina," the fairy said, reading her thoughts.

Dina didn't know the fairy could do that, which snapped her back to reality. She shuddered. "Huh? What? I don't understand."

"Oh, I think you do, Dina. You've got it right. Everything that happens from now on depends on you. So what shall it be, a drunken woman who can't find her way out when in reality, she could have avoided this awful lifestyle? It all depends on you."

"What do you mean?" Dina wondered. She looked at Odi, disappointed and lost. "The second movie was about me, wasn't it?" Her heart sank at the thought, and there was fear and despair in her eyes.

Odi glanced at the fairy. "Please tell her!" Odi was worried about his friend.

The fairy held up her hand. "Hold on, Odi," she said. "Dina, both movies were about you. So which movie would you like to be a part of?"

Dina threw up her hands. "What kind of a question is that? Of course, I want the first story, the fairy tale; it's every girl's dream. But what does it have to do with me? That story is about decent girls from good families. How could I ever be a part of that?" Her voice became muffled. "The second movie is more familiar and clearer, although I don't want to be there." She started crying, covering her face with her hands.

"Dina, it's not like that!" Odi exclaimed.

"Hush!" the fairy waved her hand. "Odi, please don't interrupt! It is not your destiny we are talking about now. It's Dina's. So tell me, child, which movie do you choose?"

"The first one!" Dina cried out and abruptly stood. Her hair was a mess, her cheeks red. "Odi, why did you bring me here? They are going to ask me demeaning questions!"

"No, Dina, listen … " Odi pleaded.

She shoved him aside. "No, I don't want to. I'm not going to listen. I've made up my mind. I said I wanted to be in the first movie, the first one! Then, after that, you can go live in the second movie if you wish!" Dina threw her arms in the air. She was boiling mad inside and felt like she was losing it.

In an instant, the fairy heard the familiar rattling at the windows. The hyenas were trying to get in. She turned her attention to them.

Odi and Dina did too and ran to the window to see. The wild pack of hyenas stood there smiling. Dina took in big gulps of air.

The fairy turned her gaze back to Dina. "If you want the first movie, you must quit your hatred and all these negative emotions and arguments, my love." However, she already knew Dina had the grit and willpower to succeed. "With these senseless outbursts, you not only encountered the hyenas but pushed your first dream move away," the fairy said. "So, that is the direct way into the second scenario of your life. All you need to do is ... ."

"Choose," Dina finished for her. "I know, Odi told me." She looked at her friend with gratitude.

Odi tried not to interrupt. The angels appeared in the back of the coffee shop. They stood there, observing Dina with anticipation.

They are always here—always, Odi thought. He looked over at Dina. It was her time now to make essential choices for her life. He should not get in the middle of it, no matter what happened. *Every human has a sacred right to freedom, purpose, and fate, and everyone makes their own choices in life.*

But, the silence was deafening.

Finally, the fairy said, "I will make some tea," and walked away toward the counter. She glanced out the window toward the hyenas but did not chase them out as she had the first time. She'd decided not to because seeing them would help Dina make a more significant effort to eliminate them herself.

Chapter 42

Dina stood there, paralyzed with inner conflict. She had a real battle going on inside her between her thoughts and feelings. After seeing the first and second movies, something was transforming deep within her soul. The hyenas outside the window reminded her about the second movie as well. The strong contrast between the two was startling and greatly impacted her thought process. There was some light in her life now, and it had room to grow at last.

The fairy returned to the table with two cups. "Drink some more hot tea, Dina. It will cheer up your spirits."

Dina automatically took the cup and sipped the tea.

The fairy took a sip of her tea, then said, "Dina, you must find the strength within yourself not to feel hatred, anger, and resentment—even towards your father, who did such a monstrous thing to you. But you won't do it for him. No, you will do it for yourself.

Feeling hatred and making a wish for revenge is

fairly easy. But if you choose that, the hyenas will eat your anger daily. They will make you even angrier, so they have more to eat. Although it will be a tasty and satisfying meal for them, you will lose your vitality daily. You will feel the weakness and the lack of drive and energy. Then you will become permanently depressed and start to feel bad physically. After that, most likely, you will be diagnosed with cancer of some sort, and it will have come full circle."

Dina was astonished. "Cancer? Because of this?"

"Yes, my dear. Have you never heard about this?"

She shifted her gaze to Odi. His face also expressed surprise at this notion.

The fairy folded her hands on the table. "Let me explain then. Your body responds to different signals coming from the brain. Cancer is old resentment downtrodden deep inside.

Infections such as Cystitis are containment of negative emotions. Allergies are the unwillingness to accept something or someone into your life, perhaps even yourself. Thyroid problems are dissatisfaction with your quality of life. Headaches may indicate unexpressed anger, self-depreciation, and regret about missed opportunities. The stomach is the seat of all emotions, so uncontrolled anger, feelings of loneliness, and envy—all provoke a response and hit different parts of this organ—also creating stomach problems.

Excess weight indicates that a person closes themselves from society or experiences internal problems such as dislike, lack of confidence in one's abilities, and experiencing a lack of attention from family, friends, and the opposite sex. So all those emotions, like anger, hatred, fear, resentment, sadness, and depression, directly affect people's physical health," the fairy explained.

Odi and Dina listened intently. Then Odi asked, "So if negative thoughts and feelings can lead to illnesses, does that mean that if a person stops experiencing them, it will lead to recovery? Even from cancer?" Odi asked.

The fairy smiled. "Absolutely, but only if it's not too late."

Dina's eyes went wide in awe of the woman before them. "All these things you're talking about are from a completely different world from ours!"

The fairy nodded. "Yes, my love, you are right! A completely different world," she said wistfully. "Yes, like different dimensions, within different corridors, but in the same reality where we all live. They never cross each other in any way. Never. It's like oil and water in different colors," said the fairy, moving her hand in the air. A holographic image of a motion bubbler appeared in her hand. "Even if you shake it, the colors will never mix. Every color will stay separate." She shook the bubbler, and the big colored oil spots broke into smaller ones without mixing. "So our world is the same; different colors are different dimensions. But there are other oils with different colors as well.

She gently rocked the motion bubbler back and forth. "In our reality, our emotions have a frequency. Negative ones have a shallow frequency, but the positives are very high. Radiating through frequencies, each person is in one or the other dimension or a frequency corridor."

Everyone was mesmerized as the tiny oil particles burst into many colors. "A dimension with low frequencies is inhabited by those who radiate them, and the hyenas live and feed there. Kind and noble people full of love do not enter these corridors. No way. These dimensions are filled with the same frequencies of deceitful, vile people, evil and corrupt, greedy, cruel haters of everyone and everything. The corridors are filled with the sounds of the crying of someone's unfortunate inner child. People living in this dimension are doomed to feed the hyenas, meet low-frequency people, and relate to these vibrations and horrible events, accidents, and all kinds of troubles," said the fairy.

She set the bubbler upright on the table. "When a person begins consciously at the beginning, they already naturally experience emotions and feelings and thoughts of high frequencies. When they enter another dimension, they begin to correspond to it. In these dimensions and high-frequency corridors live kind, sympathetic, loving, compassionate people who love this world, and the world loves them. They love, support, and help each other. Indeed, there can't be hyenas there because they can't find any food, and they will explode at such high frequencies."

"Yes! I saw it myself," Odi confirmed.

"Yes, you did," nodded the fairy. "So it's so worth it to make an effort to trace all negative manifestations. Isn't it?" the fairy finished, looking at Dina.

"Yes ... it is," Dina answered, very concerned.

"I'm so glad you understand it better now, my dear." The fairy smiled. "It's now 100 percent up to you which dimension you will live in and what corridors you will walk down. It is an everyday and every minute choice. By choosing negative or positive manifestations for yourself, you either add a deposit to the account of your dream life or withdraw in favor of the second movie."

"Yes, now I see it," Dina replied.

A loud bang came from behind them. Everyone turned around. Angels were rejoicing, giving high-fives to each other, and joyfully dancing. "Ok, you got it, girl!

The fairy stood. "Well, kids, it has been a very long day, and I am exhausted," she yawned.

The kids glanced at each other. "Home?" they both said at once. Odi hunched over, and Dina got fear in her eyes, just thinking of the dangerous, nasty places they called home.

The fairy read them loud and clear. "And that's why you are going to spend the night here, if you don't mind, of course," the fairy suggested.

"We don't mind!" they shouted in unison.

Odi looked around. "But where? There's nowhere to sleep."

The fairy sighed. "Have you forgotten that I am a fairy?"

The elf chirped in from the back. "She once housed 100 elves and Santa himself, and they all fit." He'd been there the whole time, sitting as quietly as a mouse behind the bar, so the kids hadn't noticed him. But he'd been fascinated by the movie they'd been watching.

"Very well, then," the fairy replied. She snapped her fingers, and the tables and chairs vanished. The hall split into several rooms with enough space for her and each guest.

Odi and Dina felt like the coffee shop had just become five times bigger, but that wasn't possible, right? It had been a long, hard, but fruitful day. Everyone was exhausted and wanted to go to sleep.

The fairy handed Odi and Dina big, fluffy pillows. "Here we go. It's time to get some rest," she said, walking to one of the bedrooms. "You guys just pick the room you like and go to sleep. Goodnight," she said, going into a room across the hall.

Odi and Dina chose rooms next to each other (just in case) and fell asleep as soon as their heads hit the pillow.

Chapter 43

Dina's mother awoke from what seemed to be a sharp shove on her shoulder. She opened her eyes. There was no one in the room. Her husband, Dina's father, was due to be home from his night shift, but he wasn't in the room.

She sat up on her bed. She had no hangover, even though she'd had a lot to drink the night before. She'd had a vivid dream, yet she couldn't remember it. A few silhouettes lingered in her mind, but it was not clear who they were.

She glanced at her watch. It needed to be done. She suddenly had a clear understanding of what to do. Dina's mother picked up the phone and googled the local police number. "Hello, police? Something happened in my home. I'd like an officer to come over and take my statement."

Dina awoke to the delicious smell of fresh-baked pastry. She opened her eyes and couldn't remember where she was for the first few seconds. Then all the events of yesterday flooded into her brain. She thought at first that it must have been a dream. But she felt somehow different now. She got up, dressed, and tidied herself in the bathroom. Last night she'd been so tired that she'd collapsed on the bed and fell into a deep sleep.

Coming out of her room, she saw Odi, the fairy, and the elf sitting at the bar, having breakfast. The fairy stood behind the counter, and when she saw Dina, she invited her to join them. "What would you like to drink, princess?" the fairy asked, giving Dina a wide smile.

Dina was very touched, and tears glistened in her eyes. *It is so awesome to feel that someone really cares.* "Tea, please," she answered politely.

"Of course, my dear." She went to the table where the others were already seated and pulled out the chair next to her own for Dina. Then she went to prepare Dina's tea.

Dina sat down next to Odi. He was eating a croissant with custard. "How did you sleep?" he asked.

"Like a baby, bro," she replied, stretching. "I'm starting my new life today. I am so grateful for everything you all showed me yesterday. I will watch my thoughts and emotions. But what should I do when my father tries to touch me again?"

The fairy set fresh pots of tea on the table. "Well, first, you can tell him to stop. You've had to endure him because he threatened to strangle you if you told anyone, right?"

"Yes, he did," said Dina in a trembling voice.

The fairy patted Dina's hand. "Try this. Imagine the unfortunate little boy inside him and tell him nicely to stop doing this to you because it hurts and insults you. A lot of things can turn around when you completely change inside. Do you recall that you move into another dimension when you do this? So the same people may behave differently around you and eventually leave your living space."

The fairy handed Dina a cup of fragrant tea. "First, you should try to have a rational conversation with him. If he doesn't understand, you can tell him that you will go to the police and then actually do it. You never have to endure stuff like being alone again. Always ask for help. Call the police and report what is going on with your father. If you're not at home, you always see police cars, right? You can even tell a police officer in places like a grocery store or school." The fairy placed her hand over Dina's. You have never asked for help, Dina. Have you ever thought about that?"

Dina raised tear-stained eyes to hers. "I ... I am afraid of him. He's threatened me from the first time he did it," Dina cried out.

"Yes. I understand," the fairy assured her. "All rapists intimidate their victims. But in reality, they are afraid to get caught because it means hard jail time. Victims, especially young children, are scared of threats and keep silent about what is happening. But you are old enough. So why didn't you try to ask for help instead of experiencing the increased hatred and planning of revenge?" the fairy asked, looking straight into her eyes.

Dina blinked several times. She searched for the answer to the question but clearly couldn't find one.

"I will help you with the answer," said the fairy. "This is called learned helplessness. A condition of a person in which the individual does not attempt to improve their situation and doesn't try to avoid adverse events. A loss of freedom and control accompanies this; disbelief in the possibility of change and one's strength brings depression and helplessness. It's like totally giving up. A child who has been put in this position, often without realizing it, imitates the behavior of the adults who raised and hurt him and does the same to those around him. Fear, uncertainty, lack of core, spinelessness, deceit, and lack of reflection are just the consequences."

She offered Dina a plate of cookies. "The main reason is one's inability to escape the trap. Just like a spider that can't get out of its web. They are forever imprisoned there and only strive to drag others into it." As she spoke, the fairy gesticulated with her hands in the air, and from these movements, holographic, obscure images appeared, showing what she was talking about.

Odi and Dina were watching and listening, spellbound by the magic of these actions. Bright images made a great impression on Dina; her hatred suddenly subsided, and instead, pity rolled over her. This feeling warmed her up inside.

The fairy made the holograph vanish. "However, not all violence survivors will show a learned helplessness." The development of this factor is significantly influenced by how a person perceives their surrounding reality. You can always reduce the feeling of helplessness and feel in control by taking steps to change the situation because you do not deserve to go through this.

You blamed your guardian angel for never helping you. So why had you never tried to help yourself out? You could Google a victim support line or go to the police or even your teacher, but you didn't do anything because the learned helplessness syndrome paralyzed you. So now, after you've gained all this knowledge, what do your feelings look like, and what will you do?"

Dina thought about all she had learned. "I feel bad for my father because of his childhood. I try hard not to feel hatred or resentment. If I start to, I will stop myself. There's no sense feeding the hyenas and ruining my life by doing that. It makes no sense. The only person who will get hurt from it is me. I will try to talk to him when he is sober, and if he doesn't stop, I will go to the police," Dina replied.

"Exactly, my dear! You are God's creation. You are a unique soul, a special girl, and there is no one like you. You have your tasks and goals in this life. No one has the right to treat you inappropriately, cruelly, and without respect. No one has the right to hurt you or make your life miserable—not even your parents. If they don't act lovingly and protectively, it doesn't mean you don't deserve to be loved and protected! You don't belong to them! You are not a toy for them to do whatever they want. You belong to God. Your soul is precious, and no one has a right to take it from you!"

Tears came into Dina's eyes. "Yeah, when you've been treated like that, you feel like you don't deserve normal kindness," she said, as tears flowed freely down her cheeks.

"I've felt the same way all my life," Odi chimed in.

The fairy gathered them close. "Yes, my loves, I understand you. But now you know what is happening with those hurting you. So don't ruin your life by hating them."

Odi nodded. "Yes, every action of a person is either love or a cry for help. I remember your words, but now I understand what the phrase means," he said.

"Yes, my dear … you are right," the fairy replied. "You can't change the other person because you can't change their childhood, and everything done to them. But, you can change yourself and your life.

If you don't have love, support, and protection from your parents, you can give it to yourself. You can love, protect, and care for yourself, your little inner child. You have yourself! So give your little inner child love and caring from yourself as an adult. When you love and respect yourself, other people around you will behave the same way, or they will disappear from your life. And vice versa. When you don't love yourself and don't respect yourself, people around you will reflect the same thing to you like mirrors."

Odi and Dina looked at each other.

The fairy clapped her hands. "Now, let's transform the room back to the coffee shop, shall we? A large group of elves is arriving soon for breakfast, so I need to prepare food for them." So, magically, the bedrooms transformed into a coffee shop.

Odi and Dina felt that their old worlds had been transformed just like the transformed bedrooms.

Before leaving the coffee shop, the fairy looked Dina right in her eyes and said, "Everything will be fine now, I promise."

Chapter 44

D ina arrived home inspired but also devastated. She and Odi had left the coffee shop and walked slowly home on purpose; their legs just didn't want to move any faster. She opened the door. "Hi Mom, I'm home!" Inside, there was evidence of a recent fight; her mother was in the kitchen, crying.

"Mom?"

"Dina, baby. They took him. Please forgive me."

"Who, father? Who took him?" A thousand thoughts ran through Dina's head. Why was her mother asking for her forgiveness?

Her mother blew her nose with a tissue. "I called the police. He will never hurt you again." She took Dina's hands in hers. Please forgive me for not believing you, for the pain I inflicted on you, and for being mean to you. I am a horrible mother! Please forgive me. Forgive me if you can."

Dina couldn't believe it. Was this for real? She was trembling inside.

Her mother got closer but seemed to be afraid to hug her. All of this was very weird for Dina. Eventually, they both broke down in tears and embraced each other. They cried out all the years of pain, holding on to one another, crying tears of relief. Dina had never cried happy tears before.

She and her mother's inner baby girls held hands and smiled inside them. Of course, Dina and her mom didn't see any of that, but their angels did.

Chapter 45

O di was a little late for school. A teacher approached him during his break and told him he had been summoned to the principal's office. *Oh great, I don't need this right now.*

At the end of the school day, Odi made a slow trek toward the principal's office, thinking of everything that had happened over the past month, including a couple of fights and a broken locker door. As he walked, he tried to sort out being summoned to the principal's office and think up excuses to get out of being punished for something.

When he entered the room, the principal asked him to sit. "Odi, do you know your current standing in math?" he asked.

Odi looked up. "Yes, sir. I failed the last test, but may I explain? I wasn't focused on the test that day because ... "

The principal held up his hand to silence Odi. "It was the only test you've failed, and that's ok." The principal paused, thumbing through some documents.

It was the most prolonged pause in Odi's life. *Shit, this is definitely about the broken locker*, thought Odi.

" … So if we take into consideration all the other tests throughout the year, I wish to congratulate you, Odi," the principal said, looking up from the documents.

"Congratulate me?" Odi asked, dumbfounded. "For what?"

The principal removed his glasses and set them on his desk. "You are one of the best math students at this school. You know that all test results are evaluated based on government standards. Your test scores were assessed, and according to the results, you are number one in math in our school, and your total score is excellent!

At Odi's astonished look, the principal continued. "That's not all. I received a request for you to represent our school in a national math competition. But here's the best news," the principal carried on. "You have been accepted to a high school sponsored by the best university in the country, with math as your major.

Moreover, you have received a full scholarship for gifted students. You can go there as soon as the next school year starts in August. You will live on campus and study advanced math. If you accept the offer, of course."

Odi opened his mouth and instantly closed it, realizing he didn't know what to say and would look silly, sitting there with his mouth open. But he knew the answer; the only word twirling in his head was a joyful "Yes!" He wanted to burst into a happy dance in the principal's office. "Yes, sir, of course, I accept!"

Odi exclaimed as he jumped up.

The principal smiled. "First things first. Take the paperwork home for your mom to sign. Then, bring it back tomorrow."

Odi stood, took the documents from the principal, and put them in his backpack. He walked numbly into the hallway. He couldn't feel his legs, even though they kept moving him along. Everything seemed to be floating around him; his ears were ringing.

All of a sudden, his angel appeared before him. As always, he was leaning against the wall with a wide smile.

Odi was used to his constant appearances and disappearances and happily walked right by him. *I have to share the fantastic news with Dina,* Odi thought, looking for his friend.

He walked along the hallway as if moving through a fog. He replayed the movie scenes of his successful future in his head. His heart was beating sublimely, and his soul felt triumphant. It was clear now how he was going to get there.

He heard the fairy's advice replaying in his head. *"Don't worry about how you'll get there."*

"Everything is coming true!" Odi rejoiced. At that moment, he felt he'd drawn the winning ticket of life. He was happy he had believed—it had paid off for the first time. He hadn't been deceived or betrayed. He felt like he was a part of the magic now because he was the one making the choices, therefore turning on a beautiful mechanism that had brought him into a different dimension. He felt light and weightless, and his heart was filled with excitement and joy.

And although something Odi could never have

imagined in his wildest dreams had come true, he knew this was only the beginning—there was so much more to come. And knowing it elated him, and the smile never left his face.

Chapter 46

O di was so lost in his daydreams that he didn't
see Dina approaching, and they bumped heads.
"Ouch, Odi," she said, rubbing her forehead. "I've been looking all over for you. You won't
believe what happened!" Dina said excitedly.

Odi rubbed his forehead, too. "Since I also have
something unbelievable to tell you, I suggest we discuss it at the happiest place in the neighborhood.
What do you think?" he asked joyfully.

"Let's go," Dina gladly agreed, and the friends
rushed to their new favorite spot.

The napkins flew off the tables as Odi and Dina
blew into the coffee shop.

The fairy stepped directly into their path. "Whoa,
slow down, kids. "Tell me what's going on," she said,
watching the flying paper napkins zigzag to the floor.

Odi and Dina looked around and wanted to ask
her the same question. The coffee shop seemed in-
sanely busy while they'd been gone. There were not
one but five elves at the standard table.

The kids gasped when they saw through the back

window not one but five griffins.

They were each busy doing their own thing. One was shoving at the others with his nose, another was preening his feathers, the third was eating his and everyone else's lunch, the fourth was trying to drag a cat down from a tree, and the fifth was sleeping with his furry paws up in the air.

Little people were running around inside the coffee shop and everywhere else, for that matter.

"Wow, who are they?" Dina wondered, squatting to watch them.

Each little man held a household tool—brooms, sweepers, brushes, mops, and scoops. Their faces were solemn as if they were dealing with a critical task. As soon as Dina tried to touch one of them, he swung the broom so hard that dust went straight up Dina's nose, and she sneezed.

Chapter 47

Dina sneezed again. She noticed a streak of gold dust when she wiped her nose with a nearby napkin.

"See!" one of the little men yelled. "Those griffins are messy creatures, to be sure. There is a ton of garbage to be picked up in the yard, and the elves are shedding golden dust that needs to be cleaned up. And who has to do it? That's right, our goblins!" the little man with the broom and the mop complained.

"You could collect all their golden dust and sell it!" one of the goblins joked, pretending to be serious. The other goblins' laughter was musical.

Odi and Dina could not take their eyes off the busy little housekeepers. "Who and what are they?"

The fairy's laughter sounded musical. "Those are goblins, my friends," the fairy replied. "They've always been here. You just couldn't see them before!"

"If they weren't so small, I bet you we would've!" Odi joked.

The fairy smiled. "You were just unable to see them back then. Now—you can. By the way, they also live in your homes and can be a lot of help if you get to be friends with them."

Odi glanced at Dina and the fairy, "Oh, and speaking of home. I have some great news. I am leaving next month!"

Dina's smile vanished. "And this is your happy news? How? Where are you going?"

Odi pulled the papers out of his backpack and held them out for them to see. "The principal told me today that I rock at math and can study at the best university in the country's high school program next year. And I will get to live on campus, and the program is picking up all expenses," Odi said, folding his arms across his chest. He immediately laughed at his image.

"Oh, wow!" Dina gasped. "Does that mean we won't see each other ever again?"

Odi put his arm around her shoulder. "Don't worry, Dina, we'll be in touch all the time," Odie assured her.

"Oh, good!" Dina took a deep breath and smiled again.

"Congratulations, Odi," the fairy said cheerfully. "See? Miracles can happen to someone like you quickly! I am amazed! I hope it's what you wished for."

Odi smiled broadly. "Are you kidding? I couldn't even have imagined this in my wildest dreams!" Odi declared. Then he became fearful. "It's going to be a completely different environment, with completely different kinds of people. How am I going to ... " he caught himself whining.

"Odi," the elf said. "We work for the most prestigious magical divisions in the universe, but do you think we are all the same? Of course not! Everyone comes from a different part of the world. But we're on the same mission. Christmas unites us all! And you will be united with the other students by math!"

Chapter 48

The fairy clasped her hands together. "Dina, how have you been? Did you have news to share as well?" the fairy prompted.

Dina gave them a luminous smile. "Yes! My mom turned my dad into the police today," Dina shouted.

Odi let out a low whistle. He was not the only one whose life had just changed.

She folded her arms in front of her. "That's my news. Everything is in the past now. My mom and I talked. I don't know what happened, but something inside her changed. She's become the woman she was when I was a little girl. She seems like she's gone back to normal. Also, she tossed out all the liquor in the house. She always hugs and kisses me, so I've started to feel loved again."

Odi lifted her and spun her around. "Dina, do you know what this means? Life is going to be completely different for you now!"

Dina laughed. "Ok, bro, you can put me down now."

Odi happily put her back on her feet.

The fairy brought her hands to her heart. She had tears in her eyes. She thought *the most beautiful magic happens within human nature.*

Everyone got quiet for a few moments; even the goblins stopped working, feeling the magic moment.

"Well." The fairy clapped her hands. "We need to celebrate with some tea." She walked quickly behind the counter to make it. She returned with two steaming cups and set them in front of the kids.

"There's something you should know and remember. The most significant powers in the world are love, empathy, and gratitude—the ability to love everyone and everything around you. The flashlight helped you see that anger, resentment, and insecurity are within every human being. It gave you a chance to see the world from a different angle. It allowed you to change your response to events and gave you a chance to experience love and empathy for others, especially those trying to hurt you.

When people achieve this level of consciousness, they start living in a new world, consisting of little children begging for help, and feeling love and empathy for them.

Now you also know about the stinky, hungry hyenas and will consciously never give them any more food not to lose your life force and energy. So you are going to retain enormous strength and gain a lot of helpers. And what's essential is you'll gain the chance to create your new life. So your energy will remain with you and be multiplied by your many helpers.

The door to a parallel reality will open. It has always been there, as you witnessed it. The new world provides different, unexpected, unbelievable opportunities and events. It is always filled with magic and wonders that will happen more often now. People you come into contact with will either change or disappear from your dimension if they cannot stay on the same wavelength."

Odi and Dina listened carefully, sipping their tea.

Chapter 49

T he Fairy continued, "Two people sitting on the same bench, in the same physical reality, can function in different parallel realities. One is luminous, full of possibilities, and the other is a cruel, dark, dirty world filled with pain, suffering, and the always-present pack of hungry, stinky hyenas they cannot see! Those realities never cross. But they exist at the same time, always, and everywhere. So we all choose which fact we want to live in."

The fairy left for a minute and opened the door of a wood-burning oven. She brought the kids some freshly baked croissants and drizzled melted butter over them. "Now that you fully understand how it works, you will care for your emotions, thoughts, feelings, and words. If you allow yourself to spread the horrible slime of resentment, anger, blame, greed, shame, slander, abuse, criticism, insecurity, anguish, sadness, dependency, hatred, jealousy, fear, fury, irritation, and lies, the hyenas will be right there waiting. And if they keep being fed, they will drag you down from your luminous reality into their dirt and grime. All disease, from the slightest cold to more serious illnesses, is a life force and energy eaten away by negativity."

Everyone in the coffee shop was listening to her. Even the little home goblins stopped running around.

"So remember this," she continued. "Live with love and gratitude in your heart. Gratitude is essential. Be grateful in advance for all the good things that are about to happen to you. Be grateful for even the simplest things; for everything around you, every new day, each new breath, that you have your arms and legs, and that you have something to eat.

Now you know that you are not alone in this world. Invisible threads made of energy connect us all, and you will soon be able to see them and feel their connection and unity. And with each new inner child's soul saved and directive towards the light, the amount of love and light in the world will increase. And every child living in fear, misery, and suffering inside an adult with no inner light will increase the amount of evil and darkness, thus turning into food for the hungry hyenas.

When you meet an aggressive, evil, insensitive, rude adult, just imagine a crying child asking for help. Show empathy and send them to love instead of reacting to their aggression. Gift your love to others; the world will become brighter and have many happy inner children."

She wrapped her arms around Odi and Dina. "I'm sure you will teach your children all this when you have them someday. Then, you can try to convince others who need it to bring love and light into their reality. Then they will get bigger, more beautiful, brighter, lighter, and full of many wonderful helpers who will offer endless opportunities."

The fairy moved her arms rhythmically, playing with holographic images floating in the air.

Odi and Dina listened carefully. Every word the fairy said seemed to go straight to their hearts.

"Boom!" Suddenly the fairy was interrupted by the sound of shattering glass.

Chapter 50

Everyone flinched and turned around.

Odi gasped.

The elf's griffin had flown through the window with a loud bang and a screech. He'd broken the window with his beak, planting his head right inside the coffee shop. The other part of his vast body was outside in the street. His eyes were closed.

The fairy broke the silence. "I told you he'd break my window again!" She lifted her eyebrows and gave the elf a meaningful glance.

The elf had come running and slid to his knees in front of the griffin. "Are you ok, my friend?"

The griffin carefully and cautiously opened his big green eyes, squinting. Then, he looked into the elf's fearful eyes and closed them again.

The elf threw up his hands. The Griffin still lay confused at his feet. He didn't know whether he should be scared of the fairy or celebrate that the griffin hadn't died. Then, suddenly, the griffin opened his eyes and, seeing the elf, licked him on his face. It was like going through a carwash; the elf was covered from head to toe in slobber.

Odi couldn't contain his laughter any longer. He slapped his knee in delight and let out a full-bellied laugh.

Dina and the fairy joined him.

Soon everyone else burst out in laughter as they watched hundreds of goblins try to push the griffin's head back through the window.

Just then, Odi noticed a golden glow in the air. He took a closer look and realized light golden threads were extending from each person connecting them all. They reached far beyond everyone, throughout the coffee shop, and through the walls.

He looked at Dina and realized that she also saw them. They both knew now that they were connected to everyone in this room and this world by those beautiful golden threads. They both were enjoying this new colorful, warm, and beautiful world, full of happiness and love.

Odi and Dina felt the warmth around them like never before, and we were confident that everything would work out the way it was always supposed to. How this can get even better?

Afterword

I would be happy to hear your opinion of this story and whether you liked it or not. You can express any feelings you have about the story—don't hesitate to send me an email at annaparkman358@gmail.com. Especially if this story helped you, I would be happy to learn about it. You can also contact me or give feedback on the book on Instagram, @apocalyptin, and also to follow my personal account, @annaewa_parkman.

More information about the author, as well as a detailed interpretation of the techniques used in the book, decoding and interpretation of the metaphors and symbols used in the book can be found on the author's website annaparkman.com.